"This Christmas season, reflect on the holiday's true meaning by questioning it. Rich McCaskill gives us twelve questions for the twelve days of Christmas that will help the reader consider the claims of Christ. Skeptic or believer, this book will provoke your thinking and perhaps even awaken your faith."

**Tremper Longman III,** *PhD, Yale University; Distinguished Scholar and Professor Emeritus of Biblical Studies, Westmont College*

"Rich McCaskill pinpoints what makes the message of Christ so unique and compelling in a reason-based world that oftentimes deifies scientific progress. The book carefully navigates historical, logical, biblical, and scientific evidence for contemplating why we exist on this Earth, and why the role of God in the universe can't be ruled out. *Questioning Christmas* hit home for me — someone whose faith in Jesus is continually evolving and occasionally requires a few drops of reason to remind me."

**Sean Lorenz,** *PhD, Cognitive & Neural Systems, Boston University; AI Startup Entrepreneur*

"The author has come up with an accessible handbook for those who are perplexed and skeptical about Christianity. He presents his readers with a wide array of evidence to show why Christianity matters and why one should not ignore it. The book is pastoral in its approach and insightful in its content. After reading this short book, it will be difficult not to take the person of Jesus and the Christian faith seriously. If you want to know why Christianity has impacted so many people around the world over the last 2,000 years, grab this book and give it a read; it may save your life after all."

**Sookgoo Shin**, PhD, New Testament Studies, University of Cambridge; Lecturer and Dean of Students, Malaysia Bible Seminary; author, *Ethics in the Gospel of John*

"For those Scrooges who question, doubt, or ridicule Christianity and its claims, Rich unwraps twelve answers to those questions. His conversations based on science, history, philosophy, and archaeology respond carefully and confidently to modern-day skeptics. Each chapter closes with a question to ponder that will make even believers more aware of the tenets of their faith."

**Dr. Mark Wilson**, *Director, Asia Minor Research Center, Antalya, Turkey D.Litt. et Phil., Biblical Studies, University of South Africa (Pretoria)*

"Who is this book for? How about anyone who has ever wondered "Why do I matter" or "Is my life a bunch of random events"? *Questioning Christmas* unfolds in easy and understandable ways to show that you matter, you are loved, and that there is a God who is not random, whimsical, or unapproachable. McCaskill accomplishes this through reworking the Christmas carol "The Twelve Days of Christmas," with each day representing a new gift that further reveals the value and importance you hold as a created person in God's image. So go ahead and buy the book; each chapter will prove its worth in helping you make the leap."

**Michael Viser,** *Founder and President,*
*Wells for Life*

"In the spirit of C.S. Lewis, Tim Keller, and, more recently, Dr. Rebecca McLaughlin, Rich McCaskill asks and answers the most important questions of our universe. He does so deftly, carefully, and with the pastoral gentleness that reveals his years in ministry. This book will help many, Christians and non-Christians, sort out all of the competing narratives around existence, meaning, and Christmas itself."

**Justin Anderson,** *Lead Pastor,*
*Icon Church, Seattle WA*

"Rich McCaskill brings modern wonder to an ancient story. They're all here—the artists and poets, songwriters and novelists, atheists and devout, history and modernity—all in conversation around the beauty, the mystery, the miracle of life—and if you pan back a bit, you may discover your soul engaging that conversation. Whether you are not sure you believe—or you are sure you don't believe—*Questioning Christmas* is a refreshing take on the nativity narrative that all can appreciate. A delightful ride!"

**Adam Richardson,** *PhD, University of Leicester; Lead Pastor, Church at Sandhurst, Florence SC*

# QUESTIONING
# CHRISTMAS

# QUESTIONING CHRISTMAS

## 12 CONVERSATIONS FOR SKEPTICS, SOUL-SEARCHERS, AND THINKING PEOPLE EVERYWHERE

*Written by*
Rich McCaskill

**EQUIP PRESS**

Colorado Springs

# QUESTIONING CHRISTMAS

## 12 CONVERSATIONS FOR SKEPTICS, SOUL-SEARCHERS, AND THINKING PEOPLE EVERYWHERE

Published in the United States by Equip Press 5550 Tech Center Dr, Colorado Springs 80919

ISBN 978-1-951304-25-6
eBook ISBN: 978-1-951304-26-3

Manufactured in the United States of America

First Equip Press Edition, September 2020

Cover Art by Xavier Comas

**EQUIP PRESS**

*Colorado Springs*

*For Erin who stuck by my side all these years,*
*and whose intelligence and wit make life*
*sweeter than honey*

# CONTENTS

**Chapter 11:**

**Chapter 12 :**

## INTRODUCTION

Virgins giving birth? Angels serenading shepherds? Mystical stars magically appearing? Is this stuff for real?

Much about Christmas sounds more like a fairy tale than recorded history. No wonder modern people find it difficult to believe. And this isn't all that is wrong with the story.

I asked my two teenagers what their classmates thought of Christianity. They said their friends see Christians as a hateful group who are intellectually deficient (in their words 'stupid') for believing in something which has no evidence to support it. One of them has a friend with a one-word screen saver on her phone that reads 'Jesus.' When my daughter asked about this, her friend smiled and said, "It just makes me laugh." At best, Christians are branded misguided and gullible, and, at worst, they are seen as enemies of peace and harmony in our diverse world.

*Questioning Christmas* is written for people like this who are unsure about faith but who cannot deny we have been given a remarkably unique and complex genetic code, a moral compass, and a sense that human beings have unalterable dignity. Each of these things is a gift, but from whom, and to what end?

Using the familiar Christmas song, *The 12 Days of Christmas,* we will consider each of these facts as if they were gifts from our true Love. Each chapter opens a new gift and concludes with a thoughtful question to help us pause and ponder. These questions are for all of us, for skeptics and soul-searchers, for believers and doubters alike. Each one is like a bread crumb left to lead us home.

These discoveries have meant a lot to me in my own journey of doubt. Believe it or not, Jesus welcomed skeptics and pointed them toward concrete evidence. He did not expect those who were searching for truth to believe him blindly. His true followers today do the same with the thinking people and skeptics we know. Our answer when our friends disagree with us is never—"It's true because I say it's true!" Although living by blind faith is how Christians are portrayed in our culture, this kind of assertionism is manipulation, and it has no place in a life of authentic faith. We come to Christ with our minds or we don't come at all.

Christian writers, such as Justin Martyr, Saint Augustine, and others through the centuries, have maintained that their faith is not only reasonable and rational but that it makes better sense of the facts before us than any other worldview offered. These 12 evidentiary discoveries raise questions that we all have to wrestle with. When considered, these facts will help you see why thinking people find it plausible to entrust themselves to a Jewish carpenter who walked the dusty streets of Jerusalem two thousand years ago.

We live in a culture that has greatly benefited from the scientific method, so let's be scientific in the way we go about forming our religious convictions. Consider the evidence. Be thoughtful. Don't settle for an unexamined life.

You must decide for yourself, in your own time, where the evidence leads. *Questioning Christmas* will help you see that Christian faith is not baseless ignorance. It is not a blind faith. In fact, following Jesus requires us to open our eyes to new data and use our capacity for reason as much as our heart.

If you are an open-minded person, then take this journey.

If you are a spiritually curious person, unsure about faith but looking for meaning in life, then take this journey.

If you are willing to hear the evidence for this global faith, then take this journey.

Take it one chapter a day and one day at a time, beginning today. Consider the possibility that there is more to Jesus than you may have realized.

Who knows?! You may experience the hope and joy that everyone seems to be singing about. Or you may simply become more informed about the beliefs of your Christian friends. Either way, we hope you will enjoy *Questioning Christmas* and these twelve conversations for thinking people everywhere.

# 1

A WRITER FOR MY CODE

*O*n the 1st Day of Christmas, my true love gave to me:
*A Writer for My Code*

If the advances of molecular biology have taught us
anything over the last century, it is that we are coded beings.
When Crick and Watson discovered the double helix structure
of DNA, it was a breakthrough of gigantic proportions.
Their work proved that we are coded beings and eventually
won them the 1962 Nobel Prize in Physiology. The
information in DNA is stored in a code made up of four
chemical bases Adenine (A), Guanine (G), Cytosine (C),
and Thymine (T). The complete DNA instruction book,
or genome, for a human contains about three billion
base pairs.

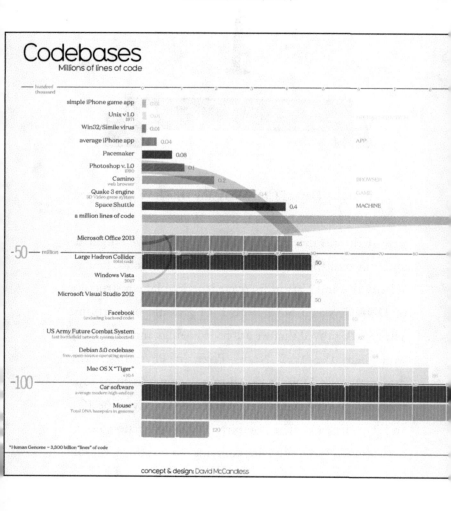

# Codebases
Millions of lines of code

| | |
|---|---|
| hundred thousand | |
| simple iPhone game app | 0.01 |
| Unix v 1.0 *1971* | 0.01 |
| Win32/Simile virus | 0.01 |
| average iPhone app | 0.04 |
| Pacemaker | 0.08 |
| Photoshop v. 1.0 *1990* | 0.1 |
| Camino *web browser* | 0.2 |
| Quake 3 engine *3D Video-game system* | 0.4 |
| Space Shuttle | 0.4 |
| a million lines of code | |
| Microsoft Office 2013 | 45 |
| Large Hadron Collider *total code* | 50 |
| Windows Vista *2007* | 50 |
| Microsoft Visual Studio 2012 | 50 |
| Facebook *(including backend code)* | 60 |
| US Army Future Combat System *fast battlefield network system (aborted)* | 63 |
| Debian 5.0 codebase *free, open-source operating system* | 65 |
| Mac OS X "Tiger" *v10.4* | 85 |
| Car software *average modern high-end car* | |
| Mouse* *Total DNA basepairs in genome* | 120 |

-50 — million

-100

*Human Genome = 3,300 billion "lines" of code

concept & design: David McCandless

Thanks to David McCandless,[1] we can compare the many lines of code required for human DNA to the lines of code needed to run popular software programs and machines. The complexity of our DNA is off the charts.

Microsoft Office 2013 requires forty-four million lines of code, and Facebook boasts over sixty million.

Behind each of these codes is a code-writer or a team of code-writers. Is it rational to conclude the same is true of our vastly more complex DNA, which contains over three billion base pairs?

Not everyone thinks so. Some look at our universe and the origin of life and think it is all the product of random chance. In his book *The First Three Minutes,* Nobel physicist Steven Weinberg explains,

This all is just a tiny part of an overwhelmingly hostile universe... this present universe has evolved from an unspeakably unfamiliar early condition and faces a future extinction of endless cold or intolerable heat. The more the universe seems comprehensible, the more it also seems pointless.[2]

---

1    David McCandless, "Millions of lines of code," informationisbeautiful. net, https://tinyurl.com/y28ty3o2 (last accessed September 9, 2019).

2    Steven Weinberg, *The First Three Minutes: A Modern View of the Origin of the Universe* (New York: Basic Books, 1977), 154.

But believing the complex code of our DNA arrived here by sheer chance is like believing you can give a typewriter to a monkey and it will eventually reproduce the works of Shakespeare.

Such a scenario stretches our beliefs in the power of random chance to the point of absurdity. Is it true, as French Mathematician Émile Borel posited, that a million monkeys with a million typewriters working a million years would eventually reproduce some of the best works of the world's greatest libraries?

In 2003, the Paignton Zoo tested this theory by placing a keyboard connected to a PC into the cage of six crested macaques.

"After a month the monkeys had produced five pages of the letter 'S' and had broken the keyboard."[3]

---

3    BBC News, "Virtual monkeys write Shakespeare," BBC.com, September 26, 2011, https://www.bbc.com/news/technology-15060310.

*Photo Credit: Tim Easley*

Complex code comes from a code-writer. Even a secular scientist like Sean Carroll sees this. In his book, *The Big Picture*, Carroll, who is a theoretical physicist at the California Institute of Technology, admits, "It's a bit of a leap, in the face of all our commonsense experience, to think that life can simply start up out of non-life, or that our experience of consciousness needs no more ingredients than atoms obeying the laws of physics."[4]

---

4    Sean Carroll, *The Big Picture; on the Origins of Life, Meaning and the Universe Itself* (New York: Dutton, 2016), 13.

When CNN interviewed Dr. Francis Collins, the head of the Human Genome project, they discovered that he had no problem with the idea of a code-writer. In fact, he calls the code in our DNA "the language of God." In his interview, he explains,

> As the director of the Human Genome Project, I have led a consortium of scientists to read out the 3.1 billion letters of the human genome, our own DNA instruction book. As a believer, I see DNA, the information molecule of all living things, as God's language, and the elegance and complexity of our own bodies and the rest of nature as a reflection of God's plan.

> I have found there is a wonderful harmony in the complementary truths of science and faith…
> The God of the Bible is also the God of the genome. God can be found in the cathedral or in the laboratory. [5]

---

5      CNN News, "Collins: Why this scientist believes in God," CNN. com, April 6, 2007, http://www.cnn.com/2007/US/04/03/collins. commentary/index.html.

Collins and other scientists have taken the rational step of reasoning from the complexity of three billion lines of code to a code-writer.

But what about us?

How else do we account for our code?

Jesus did not think human beings got here by accident. In his view, human beings do have a designer. He puts it simply—"God made them."[6] The same one who designed the stars also wrote our code, and, thus, we do have a purpose. Our code is not a randomly generated sequence without meaning or purpose. Life is not a "tale told by an idiot full of sound and fury, signifying nothing."[7] Do you prefer to see your code as something that randomly assembled itself out of nothingness? Does that not seem like believing the space shuttle assembled itself from spare parts lying around Cape Canaveral?

What if you have a designer? What if your face, your skills, your height, your gender, your dreams, and your abilities are all a gift from your code-writer? According to the Bible, that code-writer is the Creator of the Universe,

---

6        Mark 10:6.
7        Macbeth Act 5, scene 5, lines 16-27.

and when he wrote your code, he inserted his own image and likeness so you would be a unique masterpiece. Whether you agree your code originated in this way or not, this is the first piece of evidence to ponder—your complex and irreducible codedness.

You obviously have one. It allows you to comprehend these words, to ponder the reason for your own existence, and to order that double macchiato with the extra foam.

## TODAY'S QUESTION TO PONDER

Where did your code come from and why do you have it?

# QUESTIONING CHRISTMAS

# 2

## MODERN SCIENCE

*O*n the 2<sup>nd</sup> Day of Christmas, my true love gave to me:
*Modern Science*

Yes, you read that right. One gift we can thank
Christianity for is the rise of modern science. Electricity,
antibiotics, the eradication of polio, the theory of
gravity, and a host of other advances would never have
been possible without a Christian understanding of
reality.

I know this runs counter to what you may have heard
in school or on the news, but it is true. Instead of seeing
science and faith in a cold war with each other, we should
see that they are each trying to answer life's questions but
from different perspectives. A key voice in this discussion
has been Dr. Alister McGrath, Chair of Science and
Religion at Oxford University. As he said in an interview

with NPR, "Science and religion are very different in many ways, yet they are both asking very good questions and we need answers to them both if we are to live out meaningful lives as human beings in the world."[8] *He would know since he holds three Oxford doctorates in the fields of molecular biophysics, Christian theology, and intellectual history. His most recent book, The Big Question: Why We Can't Stop Talking About God, Science, and Faith (New York: St Martin's Press), published in November 2015, is worth checking out.*

In one of his public lectures at Regent College, McGrath explained,

> We live in a world which is very suspicious of being told there is only one way of seeing things. And in many ways, this ... myth of the conflict between science and religion is saying you've got no choice...science and religion conflict. But, historians don't take that seriously anymore.

---

8      NPR, "Like It or Not, We May Be 'Meaning Junkies,'" NPR.org, November 11, 2015, https://www.npr.org/sections/13.7/2015/11/11/455573765/like-it-or-not-we-may-be-meaning-junkies.

Sure, the media is taking generations to catch up to the scholarship, but the evidence is all there for you to explain.[9]

One reason faith and science should not be considered at war is because modern science was born in a religious environment. Have you ever considered what type of environment was needed for the modern scientific method to emerge? And why did these great advances in thought take place in Western Europe and not in Central America, China, or Northern India, each of which had a rich heritage of culture and medicine?

For experimental science to emerge, it needed two foundational beliefs. First, it needed the belief that nature was not divine. Second, it needed the belief that reality was rational and predictable. In many cultures where nature was worshiped, and there was a spirit behind every object, no one considered investigating, dissecting, or manipulating the natural world. Their fear and devotion made such activities unthinkable. In

---

9     Regent College, "Science and Faith: Conflicting or Enriching?" Regentinterface.com, September 18, 2018, https://www.regentinterface.com/topics/science-and-faith/.

the same way, if a person believed the natural world was subject to change based on the whims of the gods, then he/she would not take the trouble to investigate and run experiments.

Evolutionary anthropologist and University of Pennsylvania Professor Loren Eiseley has admitted,

> The philosophy of experimental science ... began its discoveries and made use of its methods in the faith... that it was dealing with a rational universe controlled by a creator who did not act upon whim nor interfere with the forces He had set in operation. ... science, which professionally has little to do with faith, owes its origins to an act of faith that the universe can be rationally interpreted.[10]

Peter Harrison, then a professor of history and philosophy at Bond University in Queensland, Australia, explained:

---

10    Loren Eiseley, *Darwin's Century: Evolution and the Men who Discovered It*, (New York: Doubleday, Anchor, 1961) 62.

Strange as it may seem, the Bible played a positive role in the development of science. ...

Had it not been for the rise of the literal interpretation of the Bible and the subsequent appropriation of biblical narratives by early modern scientists, modern science may not have arisen at all.[11]

Other views of reality did not offer this unique combination of beliefs, but Christianity did. The origins story told in the Hebrew Scriptures combined a belief in the goodness of the material world with a belief in its non-divine status. By claiming that the physical universe was the invention of a rational creator, Judaism provided the belief that reality was rational and capable of being understood. Christianity continued and strengthened these ideas and created the needed soil for modern science to develop.

The rise of modern science did not conflict with what the Bible teaches. Indeed, at crucial points, the

---

11    Peter Harrison, "The Bible and the Rise of Science," *Australasian Science* 23, no. 3 (2002): 14-15.

scientific revolution has rested upon what the Bible teaches.

Both Alfred North Whitehead (1861-1947) and J. Robert Oppenheimer (1904-1967) have stressed that modern science was born out of the Christian worldview, though neither of them were Christians nor claimed to be. Whitehead was a British mathematician and philosopher best known for his work in mathematical logic and the philosophy of science. In collaboration with famed atheist Bertrand Russell, he co-authored the landmark three-volume *Principia Mathematica* (1910, 1912, 1913). While a professor of philosophy at Harvard 1924-1937, he gave the Lowell Lectures where he claimed, "The scientific movement. ... there seems but one source for its origin. It must come from the medieval insistence on the rationality of God."[12]

Oppenheimer was a theoretical physicist who taught at UC Berkley and the California Institute of Technology. He wrestled with the question of the origin of modern science and came to the same conclusion. He wrote,

---

12    Alfred North Whitehead, *Science and the Modern World, Lowell Lectures 1925* (New York: Macmillan, 1967), 13.

It took something that was not present in Chinese civilization…, absent in Indian civilization, and absent from Greco-Roman civilization. It needed an idea of progress, … which is well expressed by the second half of the famous Christian dichotomy—faith and works…that there was the beginning of the scientific age.[13]

So for Whitehead, this underlying belief that the natural world is rational and predictable led to the scientific revolution. For Oppenheimer, it was the idea of progress offered in the Christian faith.

Another voice which has also credited Christian faith for modern science is historian Rodney Stark, who writes, "I argue not only that there is no inherent conflict between religion and science, but that *Christian theology was essential for the rise of science*"[14] (italics original). He goes on to claim that "the leading scientific figures in the sixteenth

---

13      J. Robert Oppenheimer, "On Science and Culture," *Encounter* (October 1962): 5.

14      Rodney Stark, *For the Glory of God: How Monotheism Led to Reformations, Science, Witch-Hunts, and the End of Slavery* (New Jersey: Princeton University Press, 2003), 123.

and seventeenth centuries overwhelmingly were devout Christians who believed it their duty to comprehend God's handiwork."[15]

You can see this borne out in the writings of the scientists themselves. In his letter to the Grand Duchess Christina, Galileo Galilei himself displayed a high regard for the Christian faith, and especially the Bible. He saw the physical sciences and spiritual truth as coming from the same source. He writes, "The Holy Bible and the phenomena of nature proceed alike from the divine Word, the former as the dictates of the Holy Ghost and the latter as the observant executrix of God's commands."[16] Galileo sees in the Bible something wholly true and reliable, and he affirmed, "The Holy Bible can never speak untruth— whenever its true meaning is understood."[17]

This highly respected and influential scientific mind quotes the church father Tertullian to support his argument and writes, "God is known first through nature, and then again, more particularly, by doctrine; By nature

---

15      Ibid, 123.

16      Galileo Galilei, *The Discoveries and Opinions of Galileo,* trans. Stillman Drake (New York: Anchor, 1957), 182.

17      Ibid, 181.

in his works, and by doctrine in his revealed word."[18] This view is representative of many of the scientists of that day. There was even the notion that God has revealed himself in two books—the book of Nature and the book of Scripture. Indeed, Galileo's whole tone in the letter is not to throw out the Christian faith, or to fight a battle against it, but to regard it highly and to show how it does not contradict his findings.

We see something similar in other scientists such as Robert Boyle, Daniel Faraday, and Sir Isaac Newton. They would have agreed with Einstein that "science without religion is lame. Religion without science is blind."[19] In his biography of Newton, Peter Ackroyd explains, "There was for him no necessary disjunction between science and theology. They were part of the same pursuit. Theology and science were equally avenues to God. They were the keys to true knowledge of the universe."[20] Newton's intellectual pursuits included the Old Testament, and "at his death he left a manuscript on biblical matters, incomplete, of some 850 pages."[21]

18   Ibid, 183.

19   Albert Einstein, *Ideas and Opinions* (New York: Crown, 1954), 46.

20   Peter Ackroyd, *Newton* (New York: Doubleday, 2006), 57.

21   Ibid.

His writings indicate that he saw God's involvement with the gravitational forces he had discovered.[22] In his *General Scholium*, Newton writes, "This most beautiful system of the sun, planets, and comets, could only proceed from the counsel and dominion of an intelligent and powerful Being."[23]

Read together, these statements made by leading scientists show us that the Christian view of the world at that time created the mental framework within which the entire enterprise of modern science could flourish. It made sense that, if God put things together, then we as his creatures could begin to understand how he did it. If Newton had believed that reality was an illusion or ruled by various competing deities who choose to govern them in unpredictable ways, he would never have pursued his studies.

This connection between faith and science was also important to Robert Boyle, whom many credit as the

---

22    Susan Wise Bauer, *The Story of Science from the Writings of Aristotle to the Big Bang Theory* (New York: W.W. Norton & Company, 2015), 216.

23    Sir Isaac Newton, *Newton's Principia : The Mathematical Principles of Natural Philosophy*, trans., Andrew Motte (New York: Daniel Adee, 1846), 504.

father of the scientific method.[24] Boyle's Christian faith is called "arguably the central fact of his life."[25] This faith encouraged him to explore the world around him and to run meticulous experiments, which eventually led to what we know today as Boyle's laws. As MIT Professor Ian Hutchinson explains, "Many of the great scientists—Isaac Newton, Robert Boyle, John Dalton, Michael Faraday, James Maxwell, and many others—were Christian believers who saw their science as consistent with a God who is active in the world."[26] When weighing whether to embrace Christian faith or not, this is one piece of evidence we should all consider.

---

24    Bauer, *The Story of Science*, 87.

25    Michael Hunter, *Robert Boyle Between God and Science* (New Haven: Yale University Press, 2009), 204.

26    Ian Hutchinson, *Can a Scientist Believe in Miracles? An MIT Professor Answers Questions on God and Science* (Downers Grove, Illinois: IVP, 2018), 142.

## TODAY'S QUESTION TO PONDER

Why are the laws of the natural world around us intelligible and predictable in the first place?

# 3

A MORAL COMPASS

*O*n the 3rd Day of Christmas, my true love gave to me:
*A Moral Compass*

As we saw above, modern medicine sprung up in the soil of the Christian understanding of the world.

In addition, philosophers through the years have proposed other clues that point toward the rationality of Christian thought.

One of these clues is what philosophers call *The Moral Argument*.

The Moral Argument points out that all of us have a universal sense of right and wrong and that one of the most logical explanations for this is that our Creator has put it there.

"Our most fundamental ethical commitments point toward a 'supernatural' source for our knowledge of what is good and right...Our ability to discern and love objective goodness is a gift—bestowed on us by the One from Whom all good things come."[27]

Now, granted, this is a philosophical argument, and so it may take a while to get our head around it. It does not require us to research the history of famous scientists or to study the Bible. However, it does require that we look inside and be honest about what we find there.

C.S. Lewis was a professor at both Oxford and Cambridge. In addition to philosophical and theological writings, he also wrote the Chronicles of Narnia series, which have sold over 100 million copies and spawned three major motion pictures. He openly confessed to being an atheist during his early years at Oxford. Over time, however, he reflected on this view of reality, which did not include God. He began to sense that atheism had some holes in it, which made him uneasy. The inadequacies that emerged when he saw the world from an atheistic frame of mind made him question its validity. Lewis writes,

---

27    Angus Ritchie, *From Metaphysics to Morality: The Theistic Implications of our Ethical Commitments* (Oxford University Press: 2012), 189-190.

My argument against God was that the universe seemed so cruel and unjust. But how had I got this idea…?

What was I comparing this universe with when I called it unjust? If the whole show was bad and senseless from A to Z, so to speak, why did I... find myself in such violent reaction against it? Thus, in the very act of trying to prove that God did not exist—in other words, that the whole of reality was senseless—I found I was forced to assume that one part of reality—namely my idea of justice—was full of sense.

Consequently, atheism turns out to be too simple. If the whole universe has no meaning, we should never have found out that it has no meaning: just as, if there were no light in the universe and therefore no creatures with eyes, we should never know it was dark. Dark would be without meaning.

It seems, then, we are forced to believe in a
real Right and Wrong...they are not a matter
of mere taste and opinion any more than the
multiplication table.[28]


Lewis is trying to explain that our moral sensibilities
are a clue pointing us toward belief in a moral Creator.
Every culture you encounter has this sense that some
things are right and some things are wrong. This holds true
across religious as well as socio-economic boundaries. You
can even hear it on the playground among young children.
They shout, "That's not fair!" when someone cuts in line
or steals their Oreos. But where does this ability to discern
right and wrong come from?

The Bible tells us that we are created in God's image
and likeness, and so because God is a moral being, we, his
creatures, are moral beings also.

Alex Rosenberg is brutally honest about the
implications of his atheism in his book *The Atheist's Guide
to Reality.* He writes,

---

28      C.S. Lewis, *Mere Christianity* (New York: Harper Collins, 2017), 7.

There is no such thing as... morally right or wrong.[29]

Contemporary writers in ethics, who blithely discourse upon moral right and wrong and moral obligation without any reference to religion, are really just weaving intellectual webs from thin air, which amounts to saying that they discourse without meaning.[30]

Michael Ruse, a philosopher of science from the University of Guelph, writes,

The position of the modern evolutionist . . . is that humans have an awareness of morality . . . because such an awareness is of biological worth. Morality is a biological adaptation no less than are hands and feet and teeth . . . . Considered as a rationally justifiable set of claims about an objective something, ethics is illusory. I appreciate

---

29    Alex Rosenberg, *The Atheist's Guide to Reality* (New York: W.W. Norton, 2011), 145.
30    Ibid., 7.

that when somebody says, 'Love they neighbor as thyself,' they think they are referring above and beyond themselves . . . . Nevertheless, . . . such reference is truly without foundation. Morality is just an aid to survival and reproduction, . . . and any deeper meaning is illusory.[31]

In his classic novel *The Brothers Karamazov*, Fyodor Dostoevsky paints a picture of the moral implications that can spring from this atheistic worldview. The Karamazov brothers are a diverse bunch. One is a fighter and a gambler. One is a priest. And one is a philosophy student constantly espousing a view of the universe that does not include God. Dostoevsky makes it clear that the danger of living in a universe without God is that we can begin to think no moral standard exists.

He writes, "There is no need to destroy anything, one need only destroy the idea of God in mankind that's where the business should start....Once mankind has renounced God...then the entire world view will fall of itself...the entire

---

31      Michael Ruse, *The Darwinian Paradigm* (London: Routledge, 1989), 262.

former morality."[32] The atheist brother links belief in God with the concept of absolute morals. Ivan naively believes his views of a godless universe governed by chance will lead to a better world of happiness, love, and joy But, like booking a ticket on the Titanic, in the end, his atheistic philosophy leads to tragedy.

He regularly lectures his half-brother about the absence of God and the relativity of morals but in an ironic twist of the narrative, this leads his half-brother to murder their father. What reasoning has led to the murder? Dostoevsky makes it clear when Ivan lectures on the man who adopts atheism: "Everything is permitted to him moreover since God and immorality do not exist."[33]

A similarly desperate theme is present in Cormac McCarthy's novel, *No Country for Old Men*. The story follows Chigurh, a cold-hearted and ruthless killer on the hunt for a suitcase full of drug money. His willingness to mow down anyone who stands in his way is stained even darker by his willingness to take the lives of random strangers based on the tossing of a coin.

---

32    Fyodor, Dostoevsky, *The Brothers Karamazov,* trans. Richard Pevear and Larissa Volokhonsky (New York: Alfred A. Knopf, 1992), 648.

33    Ibid., 649.

He heads into a gas station and begins interrogating the man behind the counter. He flips a coin and says,
> "Just call it...."

> The man looked at Chigurh's eyes for the first time. Blue as lapis. At once glistening and totally opaque. Like wet stones...

> "I don't know what it is I stand to win."
> In the blue light, the man's face was beaded thinly with sweat. He licked his upper lip.

> "You stand to win everything," Chigurh said. "Everything." [34]

The tension wraps around the reader like a boa constrictor, and you wonder whether this is lights out or whether the victim will be released. As chance would have it, the man behind the counter calls heads and lives to tell the tale. Later on, Chigurh uses a coin to decide the fate of

---

34    Cormac McCarthy, *No Country for Old Men* (New York: Vintage Books/ Random House, 1996), 55-56.

a young woman. She comes home to find him waiting in her house. He chats amiably with her as if it's afternoon tea even though he has a gun. While she weeps silently to herself, he reveals the worldview that has led him on his killing spree.

> She said…."You make it like it was the coin. But you're the one. It could have gone either way. The coin didn't have no say. It was just you."

> "Perhaps. But look at it my way. I got here the same way the coin did."[35]

Similar to Ivan Karamazov, Chigurh is a character who believes his life is the product of random chance. He got here the same way as the coin. This view of human origins estranges him from himself, like putting a bag over his head before looking in the mirror. It causes him to devolve into a deadly predator willing to take extreme action that hurts others.

---

35      Ibid, 257-259.

Now, to be clear, being an atheist does not make someone a murderer. You may be an atheist and be shocked at the cold heart of Chigurh and the murder of Ivan's father. This proves the point that you have a moral compass. That moral compass leads you to avoid cheating your clients at work or cheating on your spouse at home; it makes you feel guilty when you lie, and it guides many of your decisions. This moral compass is a clue to the meaning of our existence. The Christian view of reality says that you and I are the creation of a moral being. Indeed, "Morality provides powerful reasons to believe in the existence of a God who not only created and sustained the world, but whose character and nature is good and love."[36]

---

36     David Baggett and Jerry L. Walls, *God and Cosmos: Moral Truth and Human Meaning* (New York: Oxford University Press, 2016), 272.

## TODAY'S QUESTION TO PONDER

How do you explain your moral compass?

# QUESTIONING CHRISTMAS

# 4

## EYEWITNESS TESTIMONY

*O*n the 4th Day of Christmas, my true love gave to me:
*Eyewitness Accounts*

Last December, I returned from the Middle East. I had traveled there to work among Syrian refugees building a home for a widow and distributing food to displaced families. The time was heartbreaking and eye-opening.

One of the most unforgettable parts of the trip was visiting the refugees who had fled from the war in Syria. Sitting with these families, sharing coffee, and listening to them talk about their faith in Jesus was groundbreaking for me. They had grown up in predominantly Muslim contexts and suffered severe economic difficulty and displacement. And yet, through it all, they had come to believe in Jesus. They were so hospitable—opening up their homes, serving us hot Turkish coffee, and engaging in conversation.

One refugee discussed what made Jesus attractive to him. He said, "I grew up with a concept of God that was angry and distant. But then I read the Bible and I saw the humility of Jesus." He was attracted to a God who was humble enough to come down and live among his creation.

The humble incarnation of Jesus is one piece of evidence that thinking people should consider this holiday season. When you look at the religions of the world, the Christian message stands out as unique. Jesus is truly a picture of a humble God who understands the struggles and the sorrows of being human.

Nat King Cole sings about this beautifully in "Hark the Herald Angels Sing,"

> *Veiled in flesh, the Godhead see;*
> *Hail, th' incarnate Deity:*
> *Pleased, as man, with men to dwell,*
> *Jesus, our Emmanuel!*
> *Hark! the herald angels sing,*
> *"Glory to the new-born King!"*

According to the Christian faith, God took on flesh and came into our world as a real person, and his name was Jesus. Pleased as man with men to dwell. Emmanuel is Hebrew, and it is three words smashed together. To call Jesus this is to call him the "With-Us-God." Now, whether you believe that's who Jesus was or not, this claim has captured enough hearts over the centuries that now we are still singing about it two thousand years later two thousand miles away. If so many people worldwide have embraced this claim, is it wise to dismiss it out of hand? Wouldn't it be wiser to investigate it and see on what basis these claims are being adopted?

This was part of my trip to the Middle East. I wanted to explore for myself whether these people I had heard about really did worship and follow Jesus. When I got there, I was blown away at the love they had and the sincerity with which they held their beliefs even in the face of intense social pressure and persecution.

What was so attractive to my new friends in the Middle East was that, in Jesus, God was shown to be a humble king who was willing to live with his subjects.

God was shown to be like an artist who was willing to insert himself into his own art. The humility and the love this entailed warmed their hearts and made them want to know more.

Filmmakers such as M. Night Shyamalan, Quentin Tarantino, Alfred Hitchcock, and Clint Eastwood have been known to regularly appear in films which they were directing. There must be something exciting involved in trying to insert yourself into your art without overpowering it. Liu Bolin is another example of this. Liu is an artist from China known as the invisible man because he uses his body as a canvas and literally paints himself into the background of scenes he creates.

*Liu painting himself into a convenience store*

What amazing talent! In this example, we can see someone incarnating themselves into their creation. There is a parallel here with the Christian claim about Christmas and a certain manger in Bethlehem.

As C.S. Lewis wrote, "Once in our world too, a Stable once had something inside it that was bigger than our whole world."[37]

I am not sure what motivates the other artists to insert themselves in their work like this. But, for Tarantino, his movies are his passion. As he told the Telegraph, "All my movies are achingly personal."[38] He explains,

> If you're a mountain climber and your desire is to climb Everest and Fuji and Kilimanjaro—that's what you're doing. It ain't about nothing else. When you're climbing Everest you're not thinking about your bills and you're not thinking

---

37    C.S. Lewis, *The Last Battle* (New York: Collier Books, 1970),140-141.
38    The Telegraph, "Quentin Tarantino interview: All my movies are achingly personal," telegraph.co.uk, February 8, 2010, https://www.telegraph.co.uk/culture/film/7165045/Quentin-Tarantino-interview-All-my-movies-are-achingly-personal.html.

about your girlfriend,... You're thinking about Everest. That's how I feel about filmmaking.[39]

He has so much passion for his creation that it is only natural for him to make an appearance. As Jesus said, "Where your treasure is, there your heart will be also."[40] Tarantino treasures his films, and God treasured his creation. So they both follow their heart and insert themselves. The Bible tells us clearly the motivation for God's incarnation. It was his love. We were God's treasure, and so he followed his heart and came to walk among us.

But you may be thinking, *Isn't that quite a big claim? What evidence can you give me to back it up? How can I know this is truly the "With-Us-God" and not just some made-up story about a misguided rabbi who thought he was divine?*

Answer: Eyewitness accounts.

So far, the pieces of evidence we have examined, such as our genetic code, our moral compass, and the existence of modern science, have not pointed specifically to the

---

39    Ibid.
40    Matthew 6:21.

57

message of Christmas but more toward a general belief in God, which would be compatible with some sort of Creator or designer behind the universe. They are like breadcrumbs left to lead us home. If we stop with these three pieces of evidence, we may find ourselves rescued from meaninglessness or shallow pleasure-seeking, but we have not yet made it home. The next breadcrumb that must be examined is the New Testament documents themselves.

And when you look at them, you will see these texts do not read like Hansel and Gretel. They read like eyewitness accounts. In fact, this is exactly what Richard Bauckham says they are. Bauckham was Professor of New Testament Studies at the University of St. Andrews, Scotland, from 1992 to 2007. He was awarded the Michael Ramsey award in 2009 for his book *Jesus and the Eyewitnesses.*

Bauckham's work has highlighted and explained a piece of the New Testament that has often been ignored or overlooked. Similar to the physical sciences, Dr. Bauckham explored the data before him and sought to conceive of a theory that would explain all the complexities in the simplest and most elegant way, leaving nothing out. One peculiar feature in the New Testament is the use of various personal names. For instance, in Mark's account of Jesus, we read, "They compelled a passerby, Simon of Cyrene, who was coming in from the country, the father of Alexander and Rufus, to carry his cross."[41] For the average person reading Mark's account, this verse seems very matter of fact, and we read it without batting an eye.

But Bauckham pushed the pause button and asked the question. Why are we given these names here? These names do not enhance the story or move the plot along. They do not appear again in Mark's account. So why mention them by name? This was the question Bauckham sought to answer with his research.

As he opened up more passages, he discovered that there are other names sprinkled throughout the pages of the New Testament that also seem to serve little to no purpose for us modern readers. Another quick example he mentions in an interview video published by St. John's College in Cambridge is the list of Jesus' twelve disciples. These names seem important, and yet scholars have always noted that many of them do not do much of anything else significant in the narrative. We know, for instance, that

41      Mark 15:21.

Bartholomew is included in the list of names in Matthew, Mark, and Luke, but this is the only thing we know about him.

Bauckham took this data and began comparing it with other first-century writings. In his research, he discovered that naming names was a very common first-century practice done as a way of verifying the accuracy and trustworthiness of what was being written. The ancients believed in writing what was called contemporary history. That is to say, they wrote about events that you can verify with sources because the sources were still alive and well.

By mentioning these names, the New Testament writers were doing the same thing as other first-century historians. They were displaying the historicity of their accounts. It was similar to the way footnotes work today in academic circles.

They were saying in essence, "If you want to verify what I am telling you, go talk to Rufus, Alexander, and Bartholomew; they will corroborate my account." His conclusions have been groundbreaking and have gone a long way in explaining these bits of detail that seem to have no relevance to the plot for modern readers. It turns out, they are hugely relevant and point toward the eyewitness nature of these documents.

The claim that Jesus did and said things which made people think he was the "With-Us-God" did not spring up hundreds of years later, as if it was the result of a long game of telephone. It sprang up from the people who were there with him. As one of those twelve disciples later wrote, "That which was from the beginning, which we have heard, which we have seen with our eyes, which we looked upon and have touched with our hands...we have seen it, and testify to it."[42]

YouTube has a ten-minute video[43] in which Dr. Bauckham unpacks his theory. You can find it if you search for Richard Bauckham, Jesus and the eyewitnesses. It is fascinating to consider his scholarly claim. Not only has the Creator come into our world, but he has taken pains to make sure his life was recorded and entrusted to eyewitnesses. He did this so that for generations to come,

---

42    1 John 1:1-4.

43    "Richard Bauckham, Jesus and the Eyewitnesses, The Gospels as Eyewitness Testimony," *YouTube,* uploaded by StJohnsTimeline, 13 August 2009, https://www.youtube.com/watch?v=292NTf1cCNw.

skeptics and soul-searchers would not have to believe by blind faith but would have the benefit of eyewitness accounts to look back upon and consider.

One of Jesus' closest disciples reinforced this claim when he penned his letter to the other first-century believers. In the second epistle of Peter, we read, "We did not follow cleverly devised stories when we told you about the coming of our Lord Jesus Christ in power, but we were eyewitnesses of his majesty."[44]

In the post-Christmas hush, take some time to read these texts for yourself and see if you agree with Dr. Bauckham's assessment that they read like eyewitness documents. His case is compelling. If it is true, then the divine artist has inserted himself into his art—he has appeared in his own story and he can truly understand what we face in our everyday lives. If it is true, then we might want to take the time to explore what the people wrote who saw him, who touched him, who listened to him, and who felt his compassion and care.

---

44    2 Peter 1:16 (NIV).

If this is true, then he knows what you face, he understands how hard life can be, and he is here to help us make it through. If this is true, then you and I are not alone as we enter into the New Year.

On the 4th Day of Christmas, my true love gave to me eyewitness accounts of an Artist in love with his creation.

## TODAY'S QUESTION TO PONDER

How do you account for all the personal
names in the New Testament documents?

# 5

THE ROCKS CRY OUT

*O*n the 5th Day of Christmas, my true love gave to me: *Archeological Evidence*

When Jesus entered Jerusalem 2,000 years ago, crowds of disciples waved palm branches and laid their cloaks on the road as a symbol of his inauguration and their support. They celebrated and shouted, calling him a king, but others were indignant that Jesus would cause such a ruckus. His opponents said to Jesus, "'Teacher, rebuke your disciples!'

He answered, 'I tell you, if these were silent, the very stones would cry out.'"[45]

What was Jesus talking about? Why would he say the rocks should cry out?

---

45      Luke 19:39-40.

His opponents were undoubtedly familiar with Isaiah's writings and the jubilant picture they painted of God's mercy.

This is what the LORD says—
Israel's King and Redeemer, the LORD Almighty:
"I am the first and I am the last;
apart from me there is no God...

I will not forget you.
I have swept away your offenses like a cloud,
your sins like the morning mist.
Return to me,
for I have redeemed you."

Sing for joy, you heavens, for the LORD has done this;
shout aloud, you earth beneath.
Burst into song, you mountains,
you forests and all your trees,
for the LORD has redeemed Jacob,
he displays his glory in Israel.[46]

---

46      Isaiah 44: 6; 21-23 (NIV).

Like a doctor issuing a diagnosis followed by a prescription, Isaiah had diagnosed humanity as redeemed and forgiven. The accompanying prescription was for all of nature to erupt in jubilant songs and shouts of joy. When Jesus arrived on the scene, he was the fulfillment of that promise.

His disciples believed God's redemptive action was now blooming into reality before their very eyes. He was there to sweep away their offenses like a cloud and to usher in the blue skies of God's undeserved grace. This was such good news that if the people kept quiet, the trees of the forest and mountains themselves would carry the tune.

As the famous Christmas carol proclaims,

> *Joy to the earth! the Savior reigns;*
> *Let men their songs employ;*
> *while fields and floods,*
> *rocks, hills and plains*
> *Repeat the sounding joy,*
> *Repeat the sounding joy,*

Jesus' opponents found this rejoicing too hard to swallow, but Jesus embraced it.

If you can relate to the skeptics who were offended by Jesus' audacity as he entered Jerusalem, then sifting through the ancient rocks of first-century Palestine is one way to see if Jesus was a charlatan or the promised Christ. Though we cannot hear the rocks and trees clapping and singing, the uncovered ruins of first-century Palestine are not silent.

Unfortunately, many people act as if this is not the case. If we interviewed people on the street and asked why they find it difficult to believe the Christian message, what do you think they would say?

I think the majority would say, "Because there is no evidence."

As an article in the Huffington Post, by Matt J. Rossano, Professor of Psychology, Southeastern Louisiana University, stated, "A complaint often voiced by scientific atheists is that there is simply no evidence for God."[47] Famous atheist philosopher Bertrand Russell said,

---

47    Huffington Post, "Would Evidence for God Mean the End of Atheism and Christianity?" Huffingtonpost.com, December 6, 2017, https://www.huffingtonpost.com/matt-j-rossano/would-evidence-for-god-me_b_675491.html.

We may define "faith" as the firm belief in something for which there is no evidence. Where there is evidence, no one speaks of "faith." We do not speak of faith that two and two are four or that the earth is round. We only speak of faith when we wish to substitute emotion for evidence.[48]

It is unfortunate that this is the perception among many people because substantial evidence exists if you are willing to look for it. One of those pieces of evidence comes from the rocks of archeology.

In fact, archeology was one of the litmus tests that Chicago Tribune reporter Lee Strobel used when investigating the claims of Christianity. As an atheist and an investigative journalist, Lee could honestly say, "As a law-trained newspaperman, I dealt in the currency of facts—and I was convinced they supported my atheism rather than Christianity."[49]

---

48   Bertrand Russell, *Human Society in Ethics and Politics* (London: Allen & Unwin, 1954), 215.

49   Lee Strobel, *The Case for Christmas* (Grand Rapids: Zondervan, 2005), 10.

Taking all the skills he had developed working in the news industry, he began to investigate Christianity for himself. He understood the life-altering implications of the Christian message, and he wanted to look at the evidence up close and personal. That was why Strobel interviewed archeology expert John McRay, who holds a PhD in New Testament from the University of Chicago and has supervised excavation teams in Caesarea, Sepphoris, and Herodium. In 2006, he helped author *Bible Archaeology: An Exploration of the History and Culture of Early Civilizations,* and in 2008, he published the 432-page textbook *Archaeology and the New Testament.* McRay studied at Hebrew University and at the Ecole Biblique et Archeologique Francaise in Jerusalem. Strobel brought up several questions about archeology with McRay, the second of which was the existence of Nazareth. Strobel was familiar with the claims of Frank Zindler, the Director of American Atheist Press, who wrote,

> Nazareth is not mentioned even once in the entire
> Old Testament, nor do any ancient historians or
> geographers mention it before the beginning

of the fourth century. The Talmud, although it names 63 Galilean towns, knows nothing of Nazareth. Josephus, who wrote extensively about Galilee (a region roughly the size of Rhode Island) and conducted military operations back and forth across the tiny territory in the last half of the first century, mentions Nazareth not even once.[50]

McRay responds by citing Dr. James Strange from the University of Florida:

When Jerusalem fell in AD 70, priests were no longer needed in the temple...so they were sent out to various other locations, even up to Galilee. Archeologists have found a list in Aramaic describing twenty-four 'courses' or families, of priests who were relocated, and one of them was registered as having been moved to Nazareth.

50    Frank Zindler, "Where Jesus Never Walked" in *American Atheist* (Winter 1996-97), 34.

That shows that this tiny village must have been there at this time.[51]

Renowned archeologist Jack Finnegan agrees: "From the tombs [that have been excavated in the vicinity of Nazareth] it can be concluded that Nazareth was a strongly Jewish settlement in the Roman period."[52]

The validity of these claims has been bolstered by a 2009 archeological discovery reported by NBC News. Archaeologist Yardena Alexandre, Excavations Director at the Israel Antiquities Authority, was in charge of the dig.

They highlighted the significant archeological discovery of a house in Nazareth. NBC reported, "This may well have been a place that Jesus and his contemporaries were familiar with," Alexandre said. A young Jesus may have played around the house with his cousins and friends, she said. "It's a logical suggestion."[53] Ken Dark goes even further and suggests this could be the home where Jesus

---

51    Lee Strobel, *The Case for Christmas: A Journalist Investigates the Identity of the Child in the Manger* (Grand Rapids: Zondervan, 2005), 49.

52    John McRay, *The Archeology of the New Testament*, 157.

53    NBC News, "First Jesus Era House Found in Nazareth," Nbcnews. com, December 22, 2009, http://www.nbcnews.com/id/34511072/ns/ technology_and_science-science/.

may have lived.[54] The excavations of the Nazareth house enabled the scientists to deduce more about Nazareth. Their findings led them to conclude that "Nazareth was an out-of-the-way hamlet of around 50 houses on a patch of about four acres (1.6 hectares). It was evidently populated

*The Nazareth house excavation holylandphotos.org used with permission*

by Jews of modest means who kept camouflaged grottos to hide from Roman invaders said archaeologist Yardena Alexandre." This may explain why the historians that

---

54      Ken Dark, "Has Jesus' Nazareth House Been Found?" *Biblical Archaeological Review* 41, no. 2 (March/April 2015): 54–63, 72.

Frank Zindler cited did not mention Nazareth. When you are thinking about the Christian message, don't fall into the trap of thinking there is no archeological support.

A brief overview of ten archeological finds that support the reliability of the Bible,[55] has been produced by Old Testament scholar Dr. Charles Dyer. Dyer holds a PhD from Dallas Theological Seminary and has led eighty trips to the Middle East. The discussion includes the Dead Sea Scrolls, Hezekiah's tunnel, and the ossuary of Caiaphas, the Jewish high priest who condemned Jesus to death.

One particularly interesting discovery was the discovery of a stone inscription to Pontius Pilate. Though all four Gospel accounts mention him as the Roman official who condemned Jesus to crucifixion, some historians claimed his existence was a myth. However, "in 1961 at Caesarea Maritima, the city of Pilate's residence in Israel, the Italian expedition discovered a stone bearing the prefect's name."[56] In addition, Megan Broshi, who

55    "Top 10 Archeological Discoveries That Authenticate the Bible," *YouTube,* uploaded by Scriptures and Science, 3 December 2015, https://www.youtube.com/watch?v=Wo7CKYPFxDw.

56    John McRay, *Archeology and the New Testament* (Grand Rapids: Baker House Books, 1991), 204.

spent thirty years as curator of the wing of the Israel Museum housing the Dead Sea Scrolls, is credited with uncovering the stone pavement where Jesus stood before Pilate.[57]

The Bible contains different genres of literature—poetry, law, personal letters, history, biography, and prophetic prediction, to name a few. Archeology has provided an objective backdrop against which we can either substantiate or discredit the historicity of some of these texts.

Over and over again, archeological discoveries have supported the authenticity of the biblical text. One way this has happened is through the discovery of the Dead Sea Scrolls. The Dead Sea Scrolls included a scroll of Isaiah 1,000 years older than any Isaiah text researchers had examined before. After comparing this older Isaiah scroll found at Qumran with the more recent copies of Isaiah, scholars marveled at how the Dead Sea Scrolls, "Demonstrate in a forceful way how carefully Jewish scribes transmitted the text across the years."[58]

---

57    Ibid., 119.
58    James C. VanderKam, *The Dead Sea Scrolls Today* 2nd Edition (Grand Rapids: Wm B. Eerdmans, 2010), 163.

Regarding the contribution of archeology upon biblical studies, Paul Barnett concurs. He writes,

> Through archaeology we are able to fill in background details that enhance the narratives in both the Gospels and in the book of Acts. Archaeological findings have confirmed that the texts of the New Testament are from first to last historical and geographical in character.[59]

## TODAY'S QUESTION TO PONDER

How do you interpret the archeological discoveries?

---

59    Paul Barnett, *Is the New Testament Reliable?* (Downers Grove, Illinois: Intervarsity, 2003), 164.

# 6

## POWER TO FORGIVE

*O*n the 6ᵗʰ Day of Christmas, my true love gave to me:
*Power to Forgive Others*

We are halfway through our 12 Conversations for skeptics, soul-searchers, and thinking people everywhere, and we are examining a different piece of evidence each day to help you see the reasons why intelligent people find it rational to put their faith in Jesus. As we said at the beginning, Christian faith is not a blind faith. There are compelling reasons for believing. Each reason we have examined so far is like a bread crumb left to lead us a little closer to home.

We have pondered the irreducible complexity of our genetic code as humans, the rise of modern science, our moral compass, the eyewitness nature of the New Testament documents, and archeological discoveries.

Today, we consider the power the Christian faith gives people to forgive others.

To understand this, it helps to look at some of the claims Jesus made about himself. One claim made was that he had the power to forgive our sins.

In Luke's Gospel, Jesus encounters a prostitute. Luke calls her a "woman who has lived an immoral life," but Jesus tells her point-blank, "'Your sins are forgiven.' Then those who were at table with him began to say among themselves, 'Who is this who even forgives sins?' And he said to the woman, 'Your faith has saved you; go in peace.'"[60]

This offer of forgiveness is for prostitutes, tax collectors, and everyone else. In fact, when his followers begin to preach around the Mediterranean world, they said, "Everyone who believes in him receives forgiveness of sins through his name."[61]

We do not often think about this forgiveness because we feel we are pretty good people. But personal forgiveness is one of the gifts Jesus offers. To feel forgiven by God is

60    Luke 7:48-50.
61    Acts 10:43.

a great relief that brings peace to people's hearts this time of year. This personal experience gives true Christians the power to also forgive those who have wronged them.

One of the worst stories in the news a few years back was the story of Dylann Roof. Dylann was a young white man who killed nine members of a Bible Study group in South Carolina at a historic black church. When his initial hearing came up before the judge, many of the family members were there.

But shockingly, instead of anger and rage, the family members of the victims expressed *forgiveness*. This was a radical and beautiful example of how Christian faith gives people the supernatural ability to forgive others who have hurt them in the most painful ways.

The *Huffington Post*, in their article "Victims' Families Meet Dylann Roof," reports that Nadine Collier, the daughter of victim Ethel Lance, said to Roof, "I forgive you, I will never talk to her ever again, never be able to hold her again. I forgive you and have mercy on your soul. You hurt me, you hurt a lot of people, but I forgive you."[62]

---

62    The Huffington Post, "Victims' Families Meet Dylann Roof: I Forgive You and Have Mercy on Your Soul," Huffingtonpost.com, June 19, 2015, https://www.huffingtonpost.com/2015/06/19/dylann-roof-family_n_7623252.html.

Alana Simmons, granddaughter of victim Daniel Simmons, also spoke to the suspect. "Hate won't win," she said. "My grandfather and the other victims died at the hands of hate. Everyone's plea for your soul is proof that they lived in love and their legacies live in love."[63]

If we are to take a scientific approach to faith, then we must wrestle with how to account for evidence like this. A reputable news source quoted Alana Simmons and Nadine Collier saying these things. How do we account for their strange reaction to this tragedy?

How can we explain their reaction in the most simple and straightforward way?

The most straightforward explanation is that it was their faith. The power to forgive Dylann came directly from their own personal experience of Jesus forgiving them.

They were living out the verse in the New Testament which says, "Forgiving each other: as the Lord has forgiven you, so you also must forgive."[64]

Jesus' forgiveness in their lives enabled them to turn around and forgive a murderer.

---

63    Ibid.
64    Colossians 3:13.

Unfortunately, in our culture, there are a lot of negative images associated with faith. Our movies and TV shows portray faith as a thing that turns people into monsters. In Quentin Tarantino's movie *Django Unchained,* we meet one of the Brittle brothers, with Bible verses safety-pinned to his overalls while he maliciously whips a slave. Thankfully, Django stops him before he can follow through with it. But the impression left on the audience is that Christian faith leads to racism and violence. Yet compare that image with the one we are confronted with here in South Carolina. It is clear, for these people, Christian faith led them to forgiveness and mercy, even in the face of racism and violence.

The power to forgive others is a gift that has taken hold of many hearts and many homes where faith in Jesus is central. You can see it in the outpouring of forgiveness the Amish community showed in 2007 when a man went into their schoolhouse and killed their children. NPR reported that "people around the world have been inspired by how the Amish expressed forgiveness toward the killer and his family."[65] Their forgiveness even inspired them to

---

65      National Public Radio, "Amish Forgive School Shooter: Struggle with Grief," NPR.org, October 2, 2007, https://www.npr.org/templates/story/story.php?storyId=14900930.

donate money to the killer's widow and his three children. The forgiveness the Amish showed was similar to what we see in the case of Dylann Roof. It is a remarkable piece of evidence that should cause us to pause and ponder.[66]

You can also see the power to forgive others surfacing in the life of Corrie ten Boom,[67] who survived the Nazi concentration camps. After the war, Corrie encountered one of the guards from the Ravensbruck concentration camp where her sister had died. She and her sister had been sent there for hiding Jews in their home. He came up to speak to her after a public speech she gave on forgiveness. She writes,

> I was face-to-face with one of my captors and my blood seemed to freeze...

> It could not have been many seconds that he stood there—hand held out—but to me it seemed hours as I wrestled with the most difficult thing I had ever had to do....

---

66   Terri Roberts, *Forgiven: The Amish School Shooting, a Mother's Love, and a Story of Remarkable Grace,* (Minneapolis, Minnesota: Bethany House Publishers, 2015).

67   Corrie Ten Boom, *The Hiding Place,* (Ohio: Barbour, 1971).

"Help!" I prayed silently. "I can lift my hand. I can do that much. You supply the feeling."

And so woodenly, mechanically, I thrust my hand into the one stretched out to me. And as I did, an incredible thing took place. The current started in my shoulder, raced down my arm, sprang into our joined hands. And then this healing warmth seemed to flood my whole being, bringing tears to my eyes.

"I forgive you, brother!" I cried. "With all my heart!"

For a long moment we grasped each other's hands, the former guard and the former prisoner. I had never known God's love so intensely, as I did then.[68]

A handshake is a powerful act of forgiveness, and yet in October 2019, America witnessed something

---

68    Corrie Ten Boom, "I'm Still Learning to Forgive," *Guideposts*, November 1972, https://www.guideposts.org/better-living/positive-living/guideposts-classics-corrie-ten-boom-on-forgiveness.

even more profound—a hug. When Brandt Jean took the stand to face the police officer on trial for killing his brother, he must have had similar feelings to Corrie ten Boom. When we read her internal struggle, it makes the events that unfolded in that courtroom even more astounding.

Brandt Jean took the stand to share his victim-impact statement with officer Amber Guyger, who had shot and killed his brother Botham Jean. Botham was twenty-six years old and lived in the same apartment complex as Officer Guyger. He was in his own apartment eating a bowl of vanilla ice cream when Officer Guyger entered and shot him. She testified that she mistakenly entered his apartment thinking it was hers and believed he was a burglar. The prosecution said the trajectory of the bullet showed that he was either getting up from his couch or cowering when the shot was fired.

His brother's statement during the trial was unprecedented. After telling his brother's killer that he forgave her, he invited her to give her life to Christ. He said,

I forgive you…I personally want the best for you.
I wasn't even going to say this before my family,
but I don't even want you to go to jail. I want the
best for you, because I know that's exactly what
Botham would want you to do — to give your
life to Christ.[69]

This was shocking enough. But then he asked the
judge if he could give her a hug. The judge acquiesced and
the hug was heard around the world.

---

69    NBC News, "Amber Guyger sentenced to 10 years for murdering
      neighbor Botham Jean," NBCnews.com, October 2, 2019, https://www.
      nbcnews.com/news/crime-courts/amber-guyger-sentencing-resumes-after-
      murder-conviction-death-botham-jean-n1061146.

As you consider evidence that makes Christian faith both rational and believable, don't overlook this claim that it gives power for people to forgive others.

Isn't this an interesting claim? And aren't these astonishing examples of the human capacity for mercy and forgiveness? If Christianity is just wishful thinking based on blind faith, then how would you explain the power these peoples have found to forgive?

On the 6th Day of Christmas, your true love gave to you a belief system that can give you the power to forgive others.

## TODAY'S QUESTION TO PONDER

Is the power to forgive others something you would like more of in your life?

# 7

## A GOLDILOCKS PLANET

$O$n the 7th Day of Christmas, my true love gave to me:
*A Goldilocks Planet*

Do you remember the story of Goldilocks and the Three Bears? Goldilocks stumbles into a cabin in the woods to find a table with steaming hot porridge. I used to love telling this to my kids and creating the different voices for the bears. The scientific community has used this children's tale to describe our planet. We happen to find ourselves living in a part of the solar system that is neither too hot nor too cold. It is just right. And like Goldilocks, we should pause to wonder why.

In an interview with Professor John Webb of the University of New South Wales, *Australian Broadcast News* quoted him as saying, "I think it might have been my friend Dr. Charley Lineweaver and Stuart Gary who first applied the term "the Goldilocks Zone" to describe the habitable zone around a star when the temperature is not too hot or too cold."[70]

The distance of a planet from the nearest star is one factor necessary for life as we know it. If a planet is too close, then the heat from the star makes life impossible.

In the same way, if it is too far, then the planet becomes too cold to sustain life.

70    Australian Broadcasting Network, "What is the Goldilocks Zone and Why Does it Matter in the Search for ET?" ABC.net.au, February 21, 2016, https://www.abc.net.au/news/science/2016-02-22/goldilocks-zones-habitable-zone-astrobiology-exoplanets/6907836.

This is an interesting scientific fact to ponder when considering whether we are the product of random chance or not. If this was the only factor necessary for life, then it would be easier to think life spontaneously arose by chance. However, the more scientists have investigated it, the more they have discovered that being in the Goldilocks zone is just one factor among *thousands* necessary for life to form. These factors include the size of our moon, the thickness of the earth's crust, the electromagnetic force in the right relation to the nuclear force, the strong force, and much more.

In an article by the *New York Times* titled "Zillions of Universes? Or did ours get lucky," Dr. Steven Weinberg, a Nobel Laureate from the University of Texas, compared our situation to "a person who is dealt a royal flush in a poker tournament. It may be chance, but there may be another explanation—namely, is the organizer of the tournament our friend?"[71]

In 2012, columnist and editorial writer for the *Wall Street Journal*, Ben Stein, produced a movie called *Expelled*.

---

71    New York Times, "Zillions of Universes? Or Did Ours Get Lucky?" NYtimes.com, October 28, 2003, https://www.nytimes.com/2003/10/28/science/zillions-of-universes-or-did-ours-get-lucky.html.

The goal of the movie was to investigate the Royal Flush nature of life in our universe. He explores the factors needed to align for life as we know it to have sprung up in the universe. He has some interesting interviews with scientists and philosophers. One of these conversations is with renowned atheist Richard Dawkins. Toward the end of the movie, Dawkins makes the most amazing statement that perhaps life on earth was seeded from another civilization outside of our universe.

Stein: What do you think is the possibility that intelligent design might turn out to be the answer to some issues in genetics or in Darwinian evolution?

Dawkins: It could come about in the following way. It could be that at some earlier time somewhere in the universe a civilization evolved by probably some kind of Darwinian means to a very very high level of technology and designed a form of life that they seeded onto this planet. Now that is a possibility and an intriguing possibility.

And I suppose it is possible that you might find evidence for that if you look at the details of biochemistry and molecular biology. You might find a signature of some sort of designer… that designer could well be a higher intelligence from elsewhere in the universe.

Ben Stein concludes, "So Professor Dawkins was not against intelligent design, just certain types of designers, such as God."[72]

For such an outstanding atheist as Dawkins to talk in this way is surprising, to say the least. He does not use the word alien or extra-terrestrial, but that is exactly what he is talking about. It simply shows us how compelling the data pointing toward a designer must be. When he is pressed regarding the origin of life on our planet, he finds it more reasonable to posit a designer rather than to look to random chance.

When we look at all the factors necessary for our universe to exist, and for life to exist, we face a dilemma.

---

72      "Richard Dawkins on God and Intelligent Design—Expelled," *YouTube*, uploaded by Radical Truth, 25 January 2012, https://www.youtube. com/watch?v=Pckg3Kud8_A.

It seems that to believe we are the spontaneous product of random chance takes more faith than to believe that a designer beyond our world created these conditions. Jesus tells us that that designer is a benevolent being who made us in his image and desires a personal relationship with us.

Oxford professor Alister McGrath agrees: "The essential point is that if the values of certain fundamental constants which govern the development of the universe had been slightly different, its evolution would have taken a different course, leading to a cosmos in which life would not have been possible."[73]

When considering the objections that our fine-tuning came from evolution instead of an intelligent designer, McGrath quotes Charles Kingsley, who famously said, "We knew of old that God was so wise that He could make all things: but behold, He is so much wiser than even that, that he can make all things make themselves"[74] In essence, if different species are discovered to have the ability to change and evolve over time to better survive and adapt to

---

73    Allister E. McGrath, *A Fine-Tuned Universe the Quest for God in Science and Theology* (Louisville: Westminster John Knox Press, 2009), 118.

74    Ibid., 218.

their environments, then that should be further proof that the natural world has been finely tuned.

McGrath asks the question, "Is evolvability itself fine-tuned? In other words, is the capacity for Darwinian evolution, which many hold to be essential to any definition of life itself, an anthropic phenomenon?"[75] In his view, the answer is a resounding yes. He writes,

> Life ...depends upon the fundamental laws of physics and chemistry, as well as the availability of fundamental materials required to achieve certain biologically necessary outcomes...this biological process requires the availability of a stable planet irradiated by an energy source capable of chemical conversion and storage and the existence of a diverse array of core chemical elements, with certain fundamental properties, before life can begin, let alone evolve.

The capacity of evolution to fine-tune itself is thus ultimately dependent on fundamental chemical properties

75    Ibid., 180.

which in themselves can thus be argued to represent a case of robust and fruitful fine-tuning.[76]

Dawkins is familiar with the data McGrath mentioned, and so instead of ruling out fine-tuning, he grants it. However, his presuppositions about the non-existence of God prevent him from crediting these things to a divine Creator. His presuppositions lead him into the surprising leap of faith that we came from alien civilizations.

This is a danger of which we ourselves must beware. We pride ourselves on open-mindedness, so let's be open-minded.

If I found a poem written on a random piece of paper floating on the breeze around my backyard, I would not think the wind picked up a pencil and somehow pressed it against the page to create the poem. I would assume there is a poet out there responsible for it and possibly even searching for it. This logic would become even more pressing upon me if the poem was not just an inanimate piece of paper but if it could walk and talk and dance and sing. But this is exactly what we are. We are each of us intricately designed poems, dancing, singing, breathing the

---

76      Ibid., 180-181.

air, and enjoying the sunshine. Next time you watch the sunrise or take a deep breath, I hope you will stand in awe of the many factors that had to be arranged perfectly for you to enjoy those things.

And as C3P0 once said, "Thank the maker!"

## TODAY'S QUESTION TO PONDER

Where do you think the fine-tuning of our universe comes from?

## A MULTICULTURAL FAMILY

*O*n the 8th Day of Christmas, my true love gave to me:
*A Multicultural Family*

Another piece of evidence that points toward the validity of the Christian faith is its international acceptance and appeal. Other world religions are broadly mono-cultural. Yet people on every continent are found worshiping Jesus.

As Yale Professor Lamin Sanneh explains in his book, *Whose Religion is Christianity? The Gospel Beyond the West*,

> Christianity seems unique in being the only world religion that is transmitted without the language or originating culture of its founder.

Christianity has felt so congenial in English, Italian, German, French, Spanish, Russian and so on, that we forget it wasn't always so.

Christianity being a translated, and translating, religion places God at the center of the universe of cultures, implying free coequality among cultures.[77]

This is unique among the world religions, and it is one reason the message of Jesus has been accepted so far and wide.

In 2014, I spent some time studying abroad. As part of my studies, I visited the Cambridge University Library. They house a collection of Bibles from around the world in two thousand different languages. I cannot describe the feeling of walking through those stacks seeing the Christian Scriptures in Finnish, Korean, Chinese, Bulgarian, and on and on. Christianity is a global faith.

But I have seen more than just shelves of books. I have personally witnessed indigenous churches all over the

---

77    Lamin Sanneh, *Whose Religion is Christianity? The Gospel and the West* (Grand Rapids: William B. Eerdmans Publishing, 2003), 65.

globe. I have seen Christian communities worshiping Jesus with their own language and customs in the following areas:

- Nizhny Novgorod, Russia
- Beirut, Lebanon
- Reynosa, Mexico
- Nakhon Ratchasima, Thailand
- Tegucigalpa, Honduras.
- Hyderabad, India

In these communities, I have heard the message of Jesus proclaimed in Spanish, Russian, Thai, Telugu, and Arabic. In each place, even though the people have different customs, different food, and different language, there is this sense of brotherly connection and welcoming love. The hospitality of the believers in the Middle East and India especially touched me.

This is why *"Hark the Herald Angels Sing"* can proclaim:

> *Peace on earth, and mercy mild,*
> *God and sinners reconciled.*
> *Joyful, **all ye nations, rise**,*
> *Join the triumph of the skies.*

# Estimated Distribution of Christian Population by Country and Territory in 2010

*Only the 115 countries with more than 1 million Christians in 2010 are shown.*

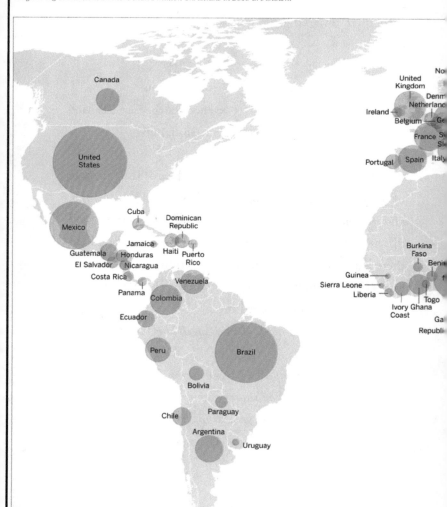

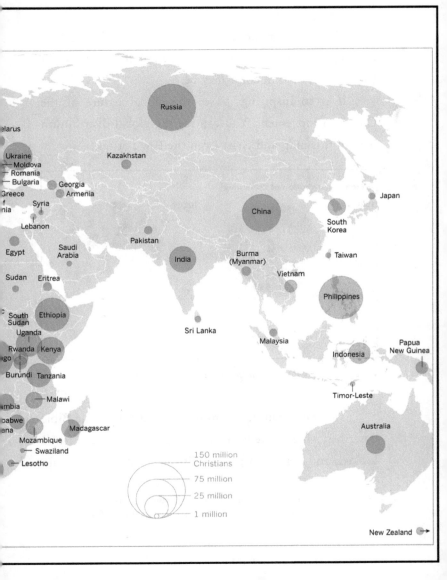

Belarus

Ukraine
Moldova
Romania
Bulgaria
Greece
...nia
Syria
Lebanon

Egypt

Sudan
Eritrea

South
Sudan
Uganda
Rwanda
...go
Burundi

Ethiopia

Kenya

Tanzania

...mbia
Malawi
...abwe
...ana

Mozambique
Swaziland
Lesotho

Madagascar

Russia

Kazakhstan

Georgia
Armenia

Pakistan

Saudi
Arabia

India

China

Burma
(Myanmar)

Vietnam

Sri Lanka

Malaysia

Japan

South
Korea

Taiwan

Philippines

Indonesia

Papua
New Guinea

Timor-Leste

Australia

New Zealand

150 million
Christians

75 million

25 million

1 million

The Christian message is joyful for all nations. All of us can join in the triumph of the skies, no matter what our background or skin color may be.

It is so inspiring to see the global nature of the Christian movement. You can see the global distribution here in this map and chart from the Pew Forum:

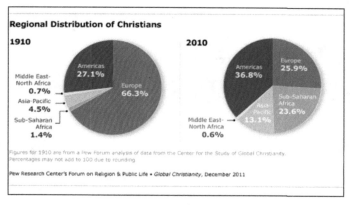

*Pew Forum Image used with permission*[78]

This multicultural community is just what the Bible describes when it tells us what heaven will be like: "I looked, and behold, a great multitude that no one could

---

78     Pew Forum, "Global Christianity," Pewforum.org, December 1, 2014,
        http://www.pewforum.org/interactives/global-christianity/#/global.

number, from every nation, from all tribes and peoples and languages, standing before the throne."[79]

This is indeed one of the most compelling reasons why thinking people should consider putting their faith in Jesus. It unifies people profoundly and transculturally.

It is exactly what you would expect to find if the God of the Bible is truly the Creator of all peoples. These believers experience faith in Jesus as a way to join a global community that transcends cultural differences.

Sanneh, who teaches at Yale, tries to explain why a religious belief system that began in the Middle East could take root and spread so widely in Africa:

> African people sensed in their hearts that Jesus did not mock their respect for the sacred or their clamor for an invincible Savior, and so they beat their sacred drums for him until the stars skipped and danced in the skies. After that dance, the stars weren't little anymore. Christianity helped Africans become renewed Africans, not remade Europeans.[80]

---

79  Revelation 7:9.
80  Sanneh, *Whose Religion is Christianity?* 43.

This may explain why there are more members of the Church of England in Africa than in England itself.[81]

> In 1970 there were 120 million Christians in Africa, estimated; in 1998 the figure jumped to just under 330 million; and in 2000 to 350 million. The projections call for over 600 million Christians in 25 years. If those projections are right—apart from South America, Africa will have more Christians than any other continent, and that for the first time.[82]

When trying to explain the rise of Christian communities in South Asia, Arun Jones, who teaches at Emory University, references the historical claims that Saint Thomas came to South India and that the Apostle Bartholomew was also involved.

> There is a general scholarly consensus that by the middle of the third century Christianity had

---

81    "Countries and Provinces," Anglican.org http://anglican.org/domain/ admin/countries.html (last accessed 11/1/2018).

82    Sanneh, *Whose Religion is Christianity*, 41.

been planted at least in South India, and was starting to sprout and grow as an Asian religious community. This Christian community saw itself as connected to the Church in Syria and Persia, and so was deeply influenced by Syrian liturgy and theology.[83]

When explaining some reasons Christianity is attractive to South Asians, he explains, "People become Christian and remain within the Christian fold because this particular faith addresses the existential questions of life's problems in ways that are compelling to them."[84] In the culture of South Asia, Christianity has been a refuge for people who have been oppressed or neglected by the majority religions. This is especially true of Indian people who come from the lower castes or the Dalit backgrounds. Whereas the dominant religion sees these people in an unalterable state of shame and guilt, the Christian message of "God's love and concern for all humanity, and the ... religious community as a fellowship of sisters and brothers

---

83    Arun Jones, *Introducing World Christianity*, edited by Charles E.
      Farhadian (Malden, MA: Blackwell, 2012), 93.
84    Ibid.

equally beloved by their Lord Jesus, ...remain appealing and compelling to those who are oppressed."[85]

In North America, we could also use some fellowship as brothers and sisters who are equally loved. Christianity offers a way for us to experience that.

This has always been a hallmark of the Christian faith from its very beginning. As Larry Hurtado explains in his scholarly exploration of the beginning of the movement, Christianity was adopted by men and women, young and old, Jew and pagan. The churches of the first centuries were remarkable in how socially diverse they were.

This major piece of evidence should lead us to ask how this message has transcended the usually impenetrable barriers of culture on such a global scale. One plausible explanation is that the God of the Bible truly is the God of the world, and his message hits home with every human heart no matter what part of the world it may be from.

---

85      Ibid., 105.

## TODAY'S QUESTION TO PONDER

Why do you think so many people from such diverse cultures have embraced Jesus of Nazareth?

# 9

## HUMAN RIGHTS

*O*n the 9<sup>th</sup> Day of Christmas, my true love gave to me:
*Human Rights*

We may not realize it, but the recognition and protection of Human Rights as we know it comes directly from the biblical worldview.

In his *New York Times* Opinion piece, Peter Wehner makes the case that we should thank Christianity for the modern understanding of human dignity.

To make his case, he quotes secular humanist and French philosopher Luc Ferry. Luc Ferry claims in his book, *A Brief History of Thought*, that in contrast with the Greek understanding of humanity, "Christianity was to introduce the notion that humanity was fundamentally identical, that men were equal in dignity—an unprecedented idea at the time, and one to which our world owes its entire democratic inheritance."[86]

On the other hand, if we take our directives from the natural world, civilization will try to base itself on the survival of the fittest. Nature does not provide us with the ideas of equality or dignity. Instead, in nature, we see might making right and the strong eating the weak.

Thanks to Jesus though, humanity has another vision to aspire to. As Wehner explains,

> Jesus' Sermon on the Mount, (blessed are the poor in spirit and the pure in heart, the meek and the merciful), his touching of lepers, and his association with outcasts and sinners were fundamentally at odds with the way the Greek and Roman worlds viewed life, where social status was everything.

> "Christianity placed charity at the center of its spiritual life"[87]

---

86    Peter Wehner, "The Christmas Revolution," *New York Times,* Dec 25, 2015, https://www.nytimes.com/2015/12/25/opinion/the-christmas-revolution.html.

87    Ibid.

We have been profoundly shaped by the Christian message and the consequent Human Rights. Our own U.S. constitution reflects this and so does the charter and existence of the United Nations.

British historian, J. M. Roberts, who has published multiple books and served as the warden of Merton College, Oxford, writes in *The Triumph of the West*, "Western civilization had an innate dynamic drive whose deepest source was its sense of direction and purpose, a confidence in its destiny as a chosen vessel. This came from Christianity."[88] Regarding slavery, he argued that the Christian worldview undercut and eventually led to the termination of slavery:

> Prominent among the ideas from late antiquity that lie at the roots of western civilization and are not found elsewhere was a certain conception of a human being. …If you believe …that the individual human soul is of infinite value, then you believe something

---

88    J.M. Roberts, *The Triumph of the West* (London: British Broadcasting Corporation, 1985), 248.

important about human equality and human claims to equality of treatment...Christianity contained a transcendent principle...a source of claims to rights. That had very long-term implications.[89]

These long-term implications led Western civilization to become the only civilization to abolish slavery "of its own internal volition."[90]

Our culture does still fall prey to greed, marginalization, and oppression. Yet the vision of a world where all humans have inherent rights and each person has equal dignity is a direct fruit of the Christian message. What would life be like without this influence? To think of a world without Human Rights is grim indeed.

In 2018, I was privileged to travel to Krakow Poland for a leadership conference. Krakow can be seen as symbolic of the human heart in that it holds historic sites of daring humanitarianism and ruthless racism within miles of each

89      Ibid., 78.
90      Ibid., 76.

other. Some memorials point toward the violation of Human Rights and some to their sanctity.

Here in Krakow, you can tour the Ghetto Heroes Square, where thousands of Jews lost their lives. Just down the street, you can walk through Oskar Schindler's factory.

*Oskar Schindler's desk preserved in Krakow, Poland*

Schindler is an example of someone who stood up for Human Rights. He is credited for saving 1,200 lives.

While I was there, I visited Auschwitz, where so many Human Rights were trampled. These atrocities break your heart when you see them. They are a striking reminder that not everyone believes in Human Rights. The Christian message calls us to never forget and to stand up for Human Rights because all people everywhere have dignity.

As the Christmas carol "O Holy Night" so eloquently puts it:

*Long lay the world in sin and error pining,*
*'Till he appeared and the soul felt its worth.*

*A thrill of hope the weary world rejoices,*
*For yonder breaks a new and glorious morn…*

*Truly he taught us to love one another*
*His law is love and his gospel is peace*
*Chains shall he break for the slave is our brother*
*And in his name all oppression shall cease.*

The reason the song can claim that oppression will cease in his name is that the Savior has been born and the human soul has felt its worth.

*Auschwitz Memorial candles outside the gas chambers not far from Schindler's factory.*

Human Rights spring naturally from the teachings of the Bible that there is a God and that he has made us in his image. When philosophers dismiss God, they run the danger of jettisoning Human Rights as well. For without the existence of God, what consistent theoretical basis is left for determining right and wrong?

As William Lane Craig has argued,

On the theistic hypothesis God holds all persons morally accountable for their actions. Evil and wrong will be punished; righteousness will be vindicated. Good ultimately triumphs over evil, and we shall finally see that we do live in a moral universe after all. Despite the inequities of this life, in the end the scales of God's justice will be balanced. Thus, the moral choices we make in this life are infused with an eternal significance. We can with consistency make moral choices which run contrary to our self-interest and even undertake acts of extreme self-sacrifice, knowing that such decisions are not empty and ultimately meaningless gestures. Rather our moral lives have a paramount significance. So, I think it is evident that theism provides a sound foundation for morality.[91]

---

91    William Lane Craig, "The Indispensability of Theological Meta Ethical Foundations for Morality," https://www.reasonablefaith.org/writings/scholarly-writings/the-existence-of-god/the-indispensability-of-theological-meta-ethical-foundations-for-morality/ (last accessed Nov 26, 2018).

As Westerners, Human Rights are part of the air we breathe. It is just common sense that everyone has rights, especially the vulnerable and minorities. And yet, if we are not careful, we can forget where this comes from. This part of our culture is a product of the Christian view of the world that, for centuries, deeply shaped our culture. I know we are grateful for it, but do we realize how this points toward the validity of Christian faith? It should at least cause us to investigate it a little further.

## TODAY'S QUESTION TO PONDER

On what basis do you believe in Human Rights and the equal dignity of all people?

# 10

**LOVE**

*O*n the 10th Day of Christmas, my true love gave to me: *Love*

Another piece of evidence that should cause us to consider the claims of Christianity is love. We talked about this earlier when we discussed forgiveness, but Christian charity is bigger than forgiveness.

In his famous essay, "Why I am not a Christian," Bertrand Russell states, "Religion is based, I think, primarily and mainly upon fear. It is partly the terror of the unknown, and partly, as I have said, the wish to feel you have a kind of elder brother who will stand by you in all your troubles and disputes. Fear is the basis of the whole thing."[92] No wonder he did not want to be a Christian.

---

92     Bertrand Russell, *The Basic Writings of Bertrand Russell,* Edited by Robert E. Egner and Lester E. Dannon (New York: Simon and Schuster, 1961), 596.

The message of the Bible, though, is not primarily about fear. No, the underlying force of the universe is love. And, according to the New Testament, Jesus was the embodiment of that love.

During Christmas 2016, Soma Eastside Church in the Seattle area tried to show love to a formerly homeless mom and her four kids. After being homeless for almost an entire year, she was able to get into an apartment of her own. As soon as people in the church heard we were trying to bless her over Christmas, they jumped into action.

People who had never met her were buying her children gifts and giving generously so we could match one of her December paychecks. We created a Facebook page called the Christmas Miracle and raised enough money to match her December paycheck. People were calling me to drop by their offices and accept donations. Another friend drove over to my house after work to shove $100 bills in my hand. It was an outpouring of love, and it was beautiful.

Does this sound like a community overwhelmed by fear? Not to me. If anything, the emotion I saw most during this time was joy and compassion. Now, where does that love come from?

In the blockbuster film *Interstellar,* there is a scene where two of the scientists are having a discussion and one of them makes the case that love is the clue to our existence.

*Original drawing of conversation between Cooper and Brand by @ _ellie_joy*

COOPER: "You're a scientist, Brand"

BRAND: "I am. So, listen to me when I tell you that love isn't something we invented—it's observable, powerful. Why shouldn't it mean something?"

COOPER: "It means social utility—child rearing, social bonding"

BRAND: "We love people who've died ... where's the social utility in that? Maybe it means more—something we can't understand, yet. **Maybe it's some evidence, some artifact of higher dimensions that we can't consciously perceive.** ... Love is the one thing we're capable of perceiving that transcends dimensions of time and space. Maybe we should trust that, even if we can't yet understand it."

There is a lot of truth to what Dr. Brand is saying.

*Interstellar* claims love is evidence that there is more to this life. Love is indispensable. It is something you have felt and something you have shown to others. This is yet another evidence that we were created in the image of a loving God and put here to love Him and to love each other. Martin Luther King Jr. was right: "There is a deep longing for the bread of love. Everybody wishes to love and be loved. He who feels that he is not loved feels that he does not count."[93]

For the skeptic who has a hard time believing in God, I have an idea for you to consider. What about devoting yourself to loving as an experiment you can run on your soul. The experience of giving and receiving love teaches us something about the nature of life and the meaning of our existence.

This is what Dostoyevsky attempts to show in a small scene at the beginning of the *Brothers Karamazov.*

A young woman is struggling with doubt in the existence of God and life after death. She comes to an old priest asking for help. She honestly admits, "I suffer from lack of faith."[94] She goes on and laments,

It's terrible! What will give me back my faith? Though I believed only when I was a child, mechanically without thinking about anything...How can it be proved?...How can one be convinced? O miserable me! ...It's devastating!

---

93    Martin Luther King Jr., *Strength to Love* (Boston: Beacon, 1963), 57.
94    Fyodor Dostoyevsky, T*he Brothers Karamazov,* 55.

The wise priest has compassion on her and responds with empathy, saying, "No doubt it is devastating. One cannot prove anything here, but it is possible to be convinced."

Immediately she is filled with hope and asks, "How? By what?"

In the priest's wise response, Dostoyevsky hands his reader a tip for spiritual breakthrough that will stand the test of time like a bottle of fine wine. She asks how she can be convinced, and he tells her,

> "By the experience of active love. Try to love your neighbors actively and tirelessly. The moment you succeed in loving, the more you'll be convinced in the existence of God and the immortality of the soul."[95]

This sparkling promise of experiencing the existence of God dangles before her, like a diamond necklace, and she wants nothing more than to have it as her own. She knows herself very well, though. She knows that loving

---

95    Ibid. 56.

others is very difficult, and so she laments again that even this simple experiment is beyond her resources to attain. She can love humanity in general, but when it comes to loving actual persons, she confesses,

> "I am incapable of living in the same room with anyone for even two days, this I know from experience. As soon as someone is there, close to me, his personality oppresses my self-esteem and restricts my freedom. In twenty-four hours, I can begin to hate even the best of men: one because he takes too long eating his dinner, another because he has a cold and keeps blowing his nose. I become the enemy of the people the moment they touch me."[96]

The wise priest shares her dilemma as the dilemma we all face, and encourages her,

> "Active love is a harsh and fearful thing compared to love in dreams. Love in dreams thirsts for

---

96      Ibid.

immediate action, quickly performed, and with everyone watching. Indeed, it will go as far as the giving even of one's own life, provided it does not take long but is soon over, as on stage, and everyone is looking on and praising. Whereas active love is labor and perseverance, and for some people, perhaps a whole science. But I predict that even in that very moment when you see with horror that despite all your efforts, you not only have not come nearer your goal but seem to have gotten farther from it, at that very moment—I predict this to you—you will suddenly reach your goal and will clearly behold over you the wonder-working power of the Lord, who all the while has been loving you, and all the while has been mysteriously guiding you."[97]

Dostoyevsky's advice is sound. Actively trying to love others, even when we fail at it, produces a reward even more precious than a strand of diamonds. It opens us up to gazing on "the wonder-working power of the Lord" and

---

97      Ibid., 58.

the most powerful force in the universe—the love of God. If we want to recover our ability to believe in something beyond what we can see and touch, then attempting to actively love others is a great first step.

As Nelson Mandela said,

Deep down in every human heart, there is mercy and generosity. No one is born hating another person because of the color of his skin, or his background or his religion. People must learn to hate, and if they can learn to hate, they can be taught to love, for love comes more naturally to the human heart than its opposite.[98]

What do you think? Does love come more naturally to the human heart than its opposite, like Mandela claims? And if so, then how do we explain that? Isn't love an intriguing reality that proves the Christian view of life is

---

98    Nelson Mandela, *Long Walk to Freedom: The Autobiography of Nelson Mandela* (New York: Little Brown and Company, 1994), 542.

accurate? After all, the Bible says that God is love and that all who live in love know God and have seen God.[99]

One thing you may not know about this book is that 50% of all the net proceeds are going directly to help Syrian refugees living in the Middle East.

These are people who have suffered greatly from the war in recent years, and many of them struggle for daily necessities like food and shelter. Even though they cannot pay us back, we want to send them help that will go toward building them better homes and putting food on the table. So far, we have built three homes in the Middle East.

Now, are you happy or sad to learn about that? My guess is that you are filled with joy that your purchase of this book helped someone you had not even met. That, my friend, is love in your heart, and it is evidence we must pay attention to if we want to figure out what life is all about.

---

99    1 John 4:16.

## TODAY'S QUESTION TO PONDER

Do you agree love is a key to understanding the meaning of life? If so, where do you think love comes from?

# UNFORGETTABLE

*O*n the 11th Day of Christmas, my true love gave to me:
*A Person I Could Not Forget*

If we trust Richard Bauckham's argument that the New Testament texts are reliable eyewitness accounts, then the next step is to investigate them for ourselves. And when you do that, you will see the person of Jesus standing out like no human being ever has. He says and does things that are unheard of. Reading them for yourself with an open mind will make it obvious why these texts have sparked such a strong reaction in the lives of billions of people around the world.

In fact, in 2013, *Time Magazine* ran an article that set out to answer the question "Who's Biggest? The 110 Most Significant Figures in History."

The authors explained, "Historically significant figures leave statistical evidence of their presence behind, if one knows where to look for it, and we used several data sources to fuel our ranking algorithms, including Wikipedia, scanned books and Google n-grams."[100]

After doing their research, they concluded that the most significant figure in history was Jesus.

Jesus unites true believers during Christmas. It is not the gifts or the music or the decorations. Those are just effects. Some of these effects remain true to the spirit of Jesus, who is the original cause. Other Christmas traditions are sadly off the mark. But the important thing is to take some time to look past those effects and get back to the original spark that caused them. Consider reading Matthew 7:1–8:17. Read Luke 15. Consider the things Jesus said and what people reported that he did. And you will see for yourself why he is such an attractive figure that recording artists from Nat King Cole, to Bob Dylan, to Mariah Carey, to Justin Bieber have had *no problem singing his praise*. Another such recording artist who still sings his praise is Bono.

Bono is not shocked that so many billions of people call themselves followers of this man Jesus. That makes total sense to him.

---

100    *Time Magazine*, December 10, 2013, time.com, http://ideas.time.com/2013/12/10/whos-biggest-the-100-most-significant-figures-in-history/.

In an interview he gave with Gay Byrne in 2013 with RTE, he explains how that all fits together. In this interview,[101] Bono explains the influence that Jesus has had on him, his family, and believers around the world.

BYRNE: "What or who was Jesus as far as you're concerned?"

BONO: "I think it's a defining question. For a Christian is who was Christ? And I don't think you're let off easily by saying a great thinker or a great philosopher. You know, because actually, he went round saying he was the Messiah. That's why he was crucified He was crucified because he said he was the Son of God. So, he either in my view was the Son of God or he was ..."

BYRNE: "Not."

BONO: "No, no ...Nuts! Forget rock and roll messianic complexes, his is like... I mean Charlie

101    "Bono: Who is Jesus?" *YouTube,* uploaded by God Inspirations, 24 March 2014, www.youtube.com/watch?v=kOQClgNRoPc.

Manson type delirium. And I find it hard to accept that all the millions and millions of lives, half the earth, for two thousand years, have been touched, have felt their lives touched and inspired, by some nutter. I just, I don't believe it."

BYRNE: "So, therefore, it follows that you believe he was divine?"

BONE: "Yes."

BYRNE: "And therefore it follows that you believe that he rose physically from the dead?"

BONO: "Yes, I have no problem with miracles I'm living round them. I am one."

BYRNE: "So, when you pray then, you pray to Jesus?"

BONO: "Yes."

BYRNE: "The risen Jesus?"

BONO: "Yes."

BYRNE: "And you believe he made promises which will come true."

BONO: "Yes. Yes, I do."

Bono may not be your favorite recording artist, but his reasoning is sound. He is also not the only artist who has come out in support of Jesus. Bono is not alone in his experience. Brian "Head" Welch, guitarist for the nu heavy metal band Korn, sings the same tune. After ten Top Twenty rock singles and six Top Ten albums, Head was struggling with addiction and depression. In an interview with *Rolling Stone,* Head talked about his transformation.

> I found Jesus, and I'm totally healed from drug abuse and alcoholism. I was in my closet doing lines, and I had a bill rolled up, and I stopped and looked at myself. And I said, "Jesus, if you're real,

please take this addiction from me. My child lost her mother to drugs — please give her one parent who's free of this. Please make me want to live." I had a bunch of eight balls, and I threw them away. Rehab didn't work; looking at my daughter didn't help me kick drugs. But I felt like I could do it finally. Miraculously, [the addiction] fell away from me within a week. I started having hope.[102]

Now he proudly displays a neck tattoo with one of the most unforgettable quotes from Jesus where he says, "Come to me, all who labor and are heavy laden, and I will give you rest."[103]

This is the same passage that stirred eighteenth-century philosopher Soren Kierkegaard in his writings. Jesus had made an unforgettable impression on him as well. He writes, "Jesus Christ walked here on earth, but

---

102    *Rolling Stone Magazine*, September 9, 2005, *Korn's Head Sees the Light: Guitarist opens up about finding Jesus, helping kids and his solo debut*, rollingstone.com, https://www.rollingstone.com/music/music-news/korns-head-sees-the-light-108203/.

103    Matthew 11:28.

this is certainly not an event just like other events. No, his presence here on earth never becomes a thing of the past."[104]

When I was sixteen years old, I encountered an unforgettable person myself. It was a dark and stormy night, and I had just finished my midnight shift in the city. I was barreling home on the wet deserted interstate in my grandmother's sky-blue Caprice Classic when it began to fishtail. Before I knew it, the rear end of the 4,314-pound Chevrolet had swung me around and I was doing sixty miles an hour backward. As I continued to spin, the driver's side met the cement median with shattering force. There I was facing north but moving southbound on I-65, with sparks of chrome and steel flying through the air past my window. Eventually, the car ground to a halt, and I sat there stunned and silent. This was before cell phones and I had no idea what to do. But that was when I met him.

He must have seen me spinning out of control and pulled over to see if he could help. Even though it was 1 a.m., and the rain was still falling, he risked his life to run

---

104    Søren Kierkegaard, *Practice in Christianity,* Edited and translated by Howard V. Hong and Edna H. Hong (Princeton New Jersey: Princeton University Press, 1991), 9.

across all three lanes of the freeway and check on me. He calmed me down and reassured me. He checked to see if the car was still drivable and then made sure no oncoming cars would hit me while he helped me make a U-turn in the middle of the interstate. I remember rumbling home with a badly deformed bumper and a crooked back tire, but at peace because of his kindness and bravery.

It was a brief encounter, but I will never forget that man who stopped to help me. But Jesus is even more unforgettable. Just searching for the hashtag #Jesuschangedmylife on your favorite social media platforms will help you hear real everyday stories from people who have found Jesus unforgettable. A number of people made selfie videos during the quarantine for COVID-19 and uploaded them for Easter. These regular everyday people from all over the world were willing to open up about the Savior they could not forget. Listening to them share the vulnerable details of their lives is inspiring.

As Rebecca McLaughlin so poignantly explains in her book *Confronting Christianity*,

Jesus…had the strength to command storms, summon angel armies, and defeat death. But his arms held little children, his words elevated women, and his hands reached out to heal the sick. Jesus drove traders out of the temple with a whip. But he tenderly welcomed the outcast and the weak.[105]

He is truly unforgettable.

So far, we have seen the message of Christmas offers us

- A Writer for Our Code
- Archeological Evidence
- A Moral Compass
- Eyewitness Accounts
- Modern Science
- Power to Forgive Others

- A Finely Tuned Universe
- A Multicultural Family
- Human Rights
- Love
- An Unforgettable Person

Next, we have…Bold Claims

---

## TODAY'S QUESTION TO PONDER

When you read the three stories Jesus tells in Luke 15, what stands out to you as unforgettable?

# 12

## BOLD CLAIMS

*O*n the 12th Day of Christmas, my true love gave to me:
*Bold Claims*

If you are not a Christian, you may or may not be
moved by some of the things we have been discussing here.
This is because of the nature of relationships.

We are not discussing here an abstract principle like
gravity or Newton's third law. We are discussing having a
personal relationship with God. And while all these pieces
of evidence are interesting, and potentially compelling, our
skepticism can still find a way to dismiss them or work
around them.

Pastor Tim Keller in Manhattan says that God's way
of convincing us is not so much to give us a watertight
argument but to give us a watertight *person*. Of course, Dr.
Keller is referring to Jesus.

To conclude our final conversation of *Questioning Christmas,* I want to thank you for considering and reading all these thoughts.

I would like to encourage you to evaluate the person of Jesus himself and the nature of his claims. During his life, he made astounding claims about himself, which are recorded in the New Testament. As Nicodemus, who was a skeptic himself, says in John's Gospel, "No one ever spoke the way this man does."[106]

But don't take my word for it. Read it for yourself.

Considering the personal claims of Jesus will require some homework on our part. Take one of the early biographies of Jesus found in the New Testament (the Gospel of Mark is a good one) and try reading it from beginning to end with an open mind. It will take you between an hour to an hour and a half depending on whether you are multi-tasking or have young children who take your reading pose as a cue to start treating your body like a jungle gym. Whatever obstacles you face, don't give up.

The question Jesus poses to Peter is the same one he poses to you and to me.

---

106    John 7:46 (NIV).

"But what about you?" he asked. "Who do you say I am?"[107]

Read the New Testament documents and try to answer that question for yourself. Who do you say Jesus is?

As you read along, look at what Jesus claims about himself.

You will see he claims things that no other human being has ever claimed.

Other religious leaders tell their followers, *I can show you the way* to God, or the way to nirvana. Jesus is unique because he says, "*I AM the way.*"[108] Other philosophers tell their followers, *I have come to teach you the truth.* But Jesus says, "*I AM the truth.*"[109] Other religious leaders tell their followers, *I can lead you to the light.* But Jesus says, "*I AM the light.*"[110]

One of his other bold claims is that he has the authority to forgive our sins. But how can a mere man have such authority?

---

107    Mark 8:29 (NIV).
108    John 14:6.
109    Ibid.
110    John 8:12.

This claim confounded his listeners and left them offended on multiple occasions. They were right when they said, "Who can forgive sins but God alone?"[111]

Jesus' claims have led many to believe that he was more than a mere man. But there are some who object. When I talk to my skeptical friends, I hear three objections more than others.

**OBJECTION #1**

One way to reject these bold claims is to say that Jesus was delusional. Maybe he made these claims because he was out of his mind and deluded by false visions of grandeur. But this theory does not explain the power he had over others. And it also does not explain how someone with a few screws loose upstairs could produce such sublime and profound teachings and parables. Teachings such as "Love your enemies ... turn the other cheek...go the extra mile,"[112] found in Jesus' sermon on the mount, have captured the hearts and minds of people in almost every culture. Does it make sense to you that they were created by a mentally unstable personality?

---

111     Mark 2:7; Luke 5:21.
112     Matthew 5.

**OBJECTION #2**

Some will object to these claims by saying that he was intentionally trying to deceive the people. They see him as diabolical, inspired by evil intent to lead people astray from reality. This is what the Pharisees and the teachers of religious law thought about Jesus. When they heard about his ministry, they said, "He is possessed by Beelzebub."[113] But the impact and character of his life was marked by compassion for the marginalized and healing for the sick. This does not sound like the work of a devil. Instead, in his wake, he left restoration, redemption, and wholeness. Again, I ask, would the devil really teach us, "Love your enemy and pray for those who persecute you"?

**OBJECTION #3**

Others will object by saying these claims are fabricated. In fact, this is probably the way most modern people avoid dealing with these claims. They say it was not really Matthew, Mark, Luke, or John who wrote these Gospels down. It was not really Jesus who said them. Instead, they say these claims were added at a much later

---

113    Mark 3:22.

date by people pretending to be Matthew, Mark, Luke, and John. Unfortunately for these skeptics, there is not enough time between the events and when they were written down for this conspiracy to take shape. Thousands of early manuscripts have been discovered, which has created a scholarly consensus that the New Testament writings were completed within seventy years of when they took place, while the people who had experienced the events for themselves were still alive to either confirm or challenge their validity.

Consider this chart comparing the manuscript evidence for the New Testament as compared to other ancient documents.

In his article published in the *Christian Research Journal*, volume 35, number 03 (2012), Dr. Clay Jones of Biola University compares the number of New Testament manuscripts with the manuscripts of other non-disputed ancient works.

| AUTHOR | WORK | DATE WRITTEN | EARLIEST MSS | TIME GAP | SURVIVING MANUSCRIPTS |
|---|---|---|---|---|---|
| HOMER | *ILIAD* | 800 BC | C. 400 BC | 400 | 1,757 |
| HERODOTUS | *HISTORY* | 480–425 BC | 10TH C | 1,350 | 109 |
| SOPHOCLES | PLAYS | 496–406 BC | 3RD C BC | 100–200 | 193 |
| PLATO | TETRALOGIES | 400 BC | 895 | 1,300 | 210 |
| CAESAR | *GALLIC WARS* | 100–44 BC | 9TH C | 950 | 251 |
| LIVY | *HISTORY OF ROME* | 59 BC – AD 17 | EARLY 5TH C | 400 | 150 |
| TACITUS | *ANNALS* | AD 100 | 1ST HALF: 850 2ND: 1050 | 750–950 | 2 + 31 15TH C |
| PLINY, THE ELDER | *NATURAL HISTORY* | AD 49–79 | 5TH C FRAGMENT: 1; 14–15TH C | 400 | 200 |
| THUCYDIDES | *HISTORY* | 460–400 BC | 3RD C BC | 200 | 96 |
| DEMOSTHENES | *SPEECHES* | 300 BC | FRAGMENTS FROM 1 C. BC. | 1,100+ | 340 |
| NEW TESTAMENT | | AD 50–100 | AD 130 (OR LESS) | 40 | 5,795 |

When you consider how many manuscripts there are and how close their date is to the date of the originals, you can see why scholars feel confident that the New Testament documents are not the product of manipulation.

Dr. Jones has done very helpful work in compiling these statistics. He concludes that the New Testament "remains in a class by itself: it is by far the most attested ancient work."[114] He also notes that "this troubles skeptics because if they reject the transmissional reliability of the NT, then they must also consider unreliable all other manuscripts of antiquity."[115]

In addition, the people who want to convince us that the New Testament claims of Jesus are fabricated have a difficult time finding a motive for such a fraud. Their writings and their beliefs concerning Jesus' claims brought threats, persecution, and, for many of them, death. John was exiled to die alone imprisoned on the Island of Patmos. Peter suffered the Roman execution of an upside-down crucifixion. And yet, even in those dire circumstances, not one of these followers of Jesus recanted. Instead, they stood by what they had written until their last breath. What they said to the religious authorities in Jerusalem rings true: "As for us, we cannot help speaking about what we have seen and heard."[116]

---

114    Jones, Clay. "*The Bibliographical Test Updated.*" Equip.org. October 1, 2013, https://www.equip.org/articles/the-bibliographical-test-updated/.
115    Ibid.
116    Acts 4:20 (NIV).

When someone tries to fabricate a falsehood, it is usually to gain money, power, or influence. And yet one of the most influential Christian leaders described his situation as follows: "We hunger and thirst, we are poorly dressed and buffeted and homeless, and we labor, working with our own hands. When reviled, we bless; when persecuted, we endure; when slandered we entreat. We have become, and are still, like the scum of the world, the refuse of all things."[117] Does this sound like someone who has gained money, power, and influence? Does it sound like someone living large and benefiting from his Christian faith? No. In fact, it sounds like the opposite.

The early Christians spread these bold claims of Jesus through oral storytelling as well as through written documents, and it brought them disdain and persecution from both their Jewish neighbors and their Greco-Roman neighbors. And yet they refused to change their tune.

To say that Jesus' claims did not come from his own lips, but were made up centuries later, does not stand up to the literary evidence. All serious scholars agree the New Testament documents were written within seventy years of

---

117    1 Corinthians 4:11-13.

Jesus' death. And to say that these claims were invented by his followers to win them power, influence, and wealth does not hold water either. We must accept the fact that these claims were written down early by eyewitnesses who heard them firsthand and who suffered for promulgating them.

Larry Hurtado, professor from the University of Edinburgh, explains that the death of Jesus proves he made bold claims. His bold claims of being more than a man, being able to forgive sin, and offering eternal life were why Jesus was accused of blasphemy. "Both synoptic and Johannine accounts of the accusations of blasphemy hurled against Jesus link the charge to offensive Christological claims that form a key component of the devotional pattern of the Christians whose experience is reflected in these accounts"[118]

What will we do with his bold claims? Maybe one of these objections sounds reasonable to you. Or maybe you have a new objection. I think the only way to find out is to read the claims for yourself.

---

118    Larry Hurtado, *How on Earth Did Jesus Become a God?: Historical Questions about Earliest Devotion to Jesus* (Grand Rapids: Wm B. Eerdmans, 2005), 155.

All thinking people have an obligation to look at the evidence for themselves and to form an intelligent and informed opinion.

On a personal note, it was my curiosity about these claims which led me to deep soul searching. I would pray and try to experience meaning in life, but it seemed there was a steel door between me and anything or anyone outside of the dark night sky of my own circular thoughts. This led me to pursue a degree in New Testament Studies. Like Hurtado, I needed to read these documents in the original languages. I wanted to investigate their claims in context, and on their own terms, for myself. As I dug deeper into the original Greek and Hebrew texts, I was struck by their authentic tone.

These were not slick propaganda pamphlets like I expected. The claims of Jesus were utterly real and surprisingly unique. But they were also subtle and nuanced.

Consider the account of Jesus walking on water. In the English Standard Version Matthew 14:27, Jesus says "Take heart; It is I. Do not be afraid." This is a comforting word from Jesus that can help us find hope in the midst of fear as it did for them. When we feel like we are out of control, this scene can give us comfort that we are not alone no matter what we are facing, whether it is a pandemic, an economic crash, a broken family, or sickness and death. But if you look in the original Greek text, you find something even more profound.

The phrase in our English Bible translated "It is I" comes from the Greek phrase *ego eimi,* "I AM." This was the name God had used of himself when he showed up to Moses in the burning bush in Exodus 3. It is also used by God in Isaiah when declaring his unique power and glory.[119] And now Jesus is using it of himself. In English, we are still impressed with Jesus' power. And in verse 33 we learn "they worshiped him," a radical act for a Jewish person who believed God was transcendent and other. But, in the Greek, when he, in essence, says, "Take heart. I AM. Do not be afraid," this reality jumps off the page even more. Jesus truly spoke of himself as God.

As Larry Hurtado explains, "Jesus' expression *ego eimi* (Matt. 14:27/Mark 6:50) is probably to be taken as an

---

119    "**I, I am he** who comforts you" (Isaiah 51:12). "**I am he**; I am the first, and I am the last. My hand laid the foundation of the earth" (Isaiah 48:12). "Even to your old age **I am he,** and to gray hairs I will carry you" (Isaiah 46:4).

epiphanic utterance, using the divine revelation formula from the Greek translation of Isaiah ."[120] Instead of a God who simply showed up in a burning bush a long time ago, this is even better, a God who dwelt in the flesh and who enters into our storms today.

As I looked at these ancient documents and wrestled with these bold claims, I found the most satisfying answer to be that they were the words of a man who was more than a man. Jesus lived with these people day in and day out, and yet they were willing not only to follow him but to worship him and to entrust themselves completely to him. What kind of a person makes that strong of an impression?

If you need a jump-start on your research, consider the bold claims Jesus makes in these passages. John 11:17-44; Luke 7:36-49; John 14:1-7; John 15:1-5.

Do not judge Jesus without first giving him a hearing and weighing his words for yourself.

---

120    Ibid., 159.

## TODAY'S QUESTION TO PONDER

What is holding you back from reading John's Gospel, highlighting every bold claim of Jesus, and pondering them for yourself?

CONCLUSION

Thank you for *Questioning Christmas* with us and joining in these 12 Conversations. Thank you also for considering the evidence that explains why thinking people find it plausible to follow Jesus in today's world. Hopefully, you discovered something new. Christian faith is not a blind faith as some have claimed. Even in the famous Christmas stories found in Matthew and Luke, the shepherds and the wise men were told to go and see for themselves why they should rejoice. As *The Shepherd's Carol* written by William Billings encourages us

> *Let all your fears be banish'd hence,*
> *Glad tidings I proclaim,*
> *For there's a Saviour born today,*
> *And Jesus is his name…*

*Seek not in courts or palaces,*
*Nor royal curtains draw;*
*But search the stable, see your God*
*Extended on the straw.*

As you head into the new year, may your fears be banished while you examine the evidence for yourself and may you experience love and meaning in your life in deeper and more profound ways than ever before. Happy New Year!

# ACKNOWLEDGMENTS

This book would not have been possible without the amazing trust and encouragement from my family and friends. Thank you to my amazing wife, Erin, for believing in this book and for helping me bring it to completion during quarantine. Thank you to my awesome kids, Ellie, Colby, Chloe, Kenzie, and Gabby for your unconditional love that stimulates me to think deeply about the meaning of life. To my parents, Dick and Kathy, and my sister, Lori, your generosity has encouraged me all my life and made it possible to believe there is still good in this world. Thank you.

Thank you to Kenny and Signe for your dedication and excellence in translating this book into Traditional Chinese so that it can reach beyond the U.S.

Thank you also to the team at Equip Press. Kara Moore and Cynthia Tucker are my heroes, and they have provided countless hours of support and guidance. I am also grateful to Steve Foster for believing in this book and getting behind it.

Thank you to my cover designer, Xavier Comas, for the iconic cover you created all the way from Barcelona. And thank you to Amy Lathrop for sharing your publishing wisdom and expertise so graciously with me.

Finally, I would like to thank my dear friend, Cass, and all my other agnostic and atheist friends. Your intelligent questions and honest searching have kept me from living a shallow life. You have inspired me to keep searching for truth, and I look forward to the day we can sit and discuss these things in person.

# ABOUT THE AUTHOR

***Rich McCaskill*** *(M.Div. Regent College)* has been privileged to enjoy many conversations with people who are unsure about faith in his work as a pastor in the Seattle area over the last twenty-two years. He helped form the leadership team of the Seattle Area Pastors Network (seattlepastors.org). And he understands how it feels to long for meaning in life when everything around us seems uncertain. His follow up book is *Questioning Jesus: 12 Unbelievable Sayings of Jesus found in the Gospel of John.* To receive a free chapter, and to engage in the Questioning Christmas Community with more questions and conversations, visit questioningchristmas.com.